Contents

Foreword

Ray Pasi has a vision of school as a caring, challenging, respectful, active center of community learning. As an administrator, he has worked closely with his colleagues to enhance and transform the schools in which they work. He has taken a leadership role in turning them into social and emotionally intelligent places where kids and adults want to be.

In *Higher Expectations: Promoting Social Emotional Learning and Academic Achievement in Your School*, Pasi shows us that he is well able to articulate the principles that have led him and his colleagues to success. This is all too rare a skill. Success does not take place through magic. It occurs after hard work, extensive planning, a high degree of focus, and an unshakable commitment to the social and emotional wellness of children. He tells us what we most need to know.

> When a school community decides to design and implement an explicit, school-wide program in social and emotional education, it is asserting its belief in a broad definition of intelligence and success, and its commitment to helping students develop their capacity to make intelligent decisions and develop healthy interpersonal relationships.

How does a school proceed? First, identify and build on what you are already doing that is a positive contributor to students' social-emotional growth. Second, recognize that effective social and emotional learning is incorporated into direct and indirect instruction throughout all areas of school life. Third, know that the climate of each classroom and the school overall must be characterized by caring and respect. This is true not only for social-emotional development but also for academic learning that children internalize and then put to use for good in their social world.

I will not enumerate all of Ray Pasi's "Rules for Schools" from Chapter 2. But reading that chapter and those that follow will leave an indelible impression. Here is an initiative supported by empirical data, blessed with numerous, accessible examples of successful implementation, supported by a growing organization, the Collaborative to Advance Social and Emotional Learning (www.CASEL.org), and rooted in a deep sense of hopefulness, respect, and caring. And Ray Pasi has the gift of being able to describe the process by which schools can transform themselves into true learning communities.

The process begins with an attitude of respectful candor, which allows staff to have small-group discussions that include reflections on both one's own and the school's SEL-related practices, on areas of strength and those needing improvement. He advocates for setting up a Steering Committee to provide leadership to the ongoing, evolving work involved in raising the SEL of a school. He talks knowingly of anticipating obstacles, and of involving many stakeholders and constituents so that the work can proceed with broad support.

Most readers will find Chapters 5 and 6 invaluable. Chapter 5 conveys school-wide activities that set a tone and an expectation for a learning environment in which students feel a genuine sense of connection to one another, to their school, and to their community. Chapter 6 focuses on how SEL can be infused into academics in such a way that it is "added in," rather than being simply "added on." Most powerful, I feel, is the use of themes. The potency of themes is confirmed by one of the fundamental principles of social emotional learning:

> Goal-setting and problem solving provide direction and energy for learning. (National Center for Education and Innovation, 1999)

Children today need something to help them organize their formal and informal learning experiences, especially considering the hecticness of their lives and the discontinuities of their school days. Themes such as Respect, Responsibility, Understanding and Treating Others Well, and Decision-Making become ways to make a powerful impression on children, transforming the learning environment from one involving struggle into one characterized by partnership, enthusiasm, and enjoyment.

I have seen such schools in action, and they are the kind of schools in which I want my own children to learn. More to the point, this is where *all* children should learn. It is their right, and they deserve it. In this book, Ray Pasi has provided the guidance needed to help schools reach the potential they have to be challenging and caring places, schools that produce children we can be proud of and who can be proud of themselves.

Maurice J. Elias, Ph.D.
Professor of Psychology, Rutgers University
Vice-Chair, Leadership Team
Collaborative to Advance Social and Emotional Learning (CASEL)

REFERENCE

National Center for Education and Innovation. (1999). *Lessons for Life video inservice kit: How smart schools boost academic, social, and emotional intelligence.* Bloomington, IN: HOPE Foundation (www.Communitiesofhope.org).

Preface

I sit at my desk in a quiet, New England town adjacent to Providence, Rhode Island. As I write, this morning's headline in the local newspaper is sad and startling: "Kids Killing Kids." In the past few weeks this small city has seen several of its young adults fight, and sometimes kill, peers who had been their friends just months—even days—before. Here, as in similar accounts elsewhere, the neighbors and friends inevitably describe the many good qualities of victim *and* assailant involved in such violence. What important qualities were missing in the young person who reacted so violently and impulsively? As educators, should we abandon hope that we can play a more significant role than we already do in preventing more tragedies?

Parents and teachers have long been aware of the need for a united effort to counter the negative effects that violence in the media, the breakdown of the family, and the ever-present realities of peer pressure have on young people. By providing children with the skills to increase their self-awareness, handle their emotions, and deal effectively with inevitable interpersonal conflicts, educators can help achieve that goal.

Consider the statistics that reflect the trouble so many young people are in today: In the United States alone, juvenile rates for violent crime reached their highest point in the 1990s; the teen murder rate quadrupled from 1980 to 1990; teen arrests doubled for forcible rape, and suicide rates tripled from 1980 to 1990; more younger teens are becoming pregnant, and venereal disease among teenagers has tripled since 1980 (U.S. Bureau of the Census, 1997).

One need not rely on statistics and countless studies, however, to uncover evidence of increased personal and social difficulties among the young. At virtually every educational conference one attends, professionals who work with children overwhelmingly attest to observing greater numbers of young people with signs of serious problems.

Social and emotional learning (SEL) education refers to the explicit nurturing of skills and attributes whose level of development helps determine the strength of our emotional competence. Children with well-developed social and emotional skills are at an advantage in every significant area of life, including, but not limited to, their academic achievement. These are the young people who feel more capable of interacting with others and more willing to accept a new challenge; who act responsibly toward others, including those different from themselves; who are more prone to engage in positive, health-producing behaviors than those that are negative and destructive.

The necessary skills to combat the problems are best learned at home, starting at a young age, from parents who teach through modeling how to get along with others, how to control emotions, how to make thoughtful, intelligent decisions. They are best learned when observed, absorbed, and lived from childhood throughout one's developing years. How their parents or guardians interact with others goes a long way toward molding children's own views of relationships.

Ultimately, society cannot expect any other outside influence, including school, to replace the role of a parent. At the same time, there is no denying that within schools, adults not related to a student—administrators, teachers, coaches—do make invaluable contributions to shaping children. Many of us can think of people in those roles who encouraged and took an interest in us when we were younger, and some of us carry the benefits of those contacts to the present.

Fortunately, many educators no longer view emotional development as an optional add-on, something to do when time permits in between more important academic work; instead, it is considered an important foundation for success in school and life. Viewed in this way, social and emotional learning are recognized as important components of intelligence, included in a school program, in part, to help enhance how well an individual uses his or her intellect.

From the start, it is wise to acknowledge that our efforts cannot solve *all* the problems facing young people or schools. Children are in school for a limited time each week, and no SEL program will ever be able to address every skill and attitude that contributes to a healthy, whole child. In order to ensure optimistic yet realistic attitudes among adults working on the development of such programs, expectations for success should not be overstated. There is increasing evidence, however, that SEL potentially contributes to improved student academic achievement, attendance, and peer relationships (Cohen, 1999; Hawkins, 1997).

Educators today are forced to balance the tension between a public that measures school success almost solely by student achievement and test scores, yet expects students to learn in an encouraging, nurturing environment. Meeting such challenges takes commitment and a long-term approach, however, as teachers work with students to ensure that their school *achievement* and *future* happiness have been enhanced by the attention given to their social skills and emotional health.

This book draws upon current theories and my own professional experience. This experience includes coordinating the design and implementation of a comprehensive program in social and emotional learning at La Salle Academy in Providence, Rhode Island, and ongoing work in this area with my colleagues at Yorktown High School and Williamsburg Middle School in Arlington, Virginia. In these settings, we have enjoyed some success, while we also have learned from the inevitable problems and challenges that arise with any initiative. It is my hope that our experiences as distilled here will further your thinking—whether you are a school administrator, teacher, or parent—about how educational institutions can enrich what they currently offer their students in the social and emotional domains.

Acknowledgments

I wish to thank the many individuals who, over the years, have assisted me with this project. First, I am fortunate to work with so many outstanding educators in the Arlington County (Virginia) school system; I am genuinely thankful for that opportunity. My colleagues at schools like LaSalle Academy, Yorktown High School, and Williamsburg Middle School, in particular, have brought the theory represented in this book to life. It is a privilege for me to have this opportunity to thank them for their example, insights and dedication.

Thank you also to the following individuals who have discussed this topic with me over the years, or have helped me to complete this project: Marilyn Taylor, Sheran Marks, Benjamin R. Taylor, Dianne Carosi, Sarah Robertson, William J. McCluskey, Kevin E. Conway, Linda Hutchinson, Peter Fazziola, Maurice Elias, and the students at La Salle and Yorktown.

Finally, thank you to Carol Collins and Karl Nyberg, editors at Teachers College Press.

HIGHER EXPECTATIONS

Promoting
Social Emotional Learning and
Academic Achievement in Your School

Yesterday, I met a whole person. It is a rare experience, but always an illuminating and ennobling one. It costs so much to be a full human being that there are very few that have the enlightenment or the courage to pay the price. One has to abandon altogether the search for security, to reach out to the risk of living with both arms. One has to embrace the world like a lover yet demand no easy return of love. One has to accept pain as a condition of existence. One has to court doubt and darkness as the cost of knowing. One needs a will, stubborn in conflict, but apt always to the total acceptance of every consequence of living and dying.

—from Morris L. West, *The Shoes of the Fisherman*

1 Introduction: The Case for SEL

Will they learn the basic skills? Will they get good grades? Will they make the varsity? Will their verbal and math abilities be strong enough for the S.A.T.? Will they get into a good school?

These are some of the questions that have long served as a measure of student success for concerned teachers and parents. Today, however, other questions have become just as important.

Will they learn how to get along with others? Will they be smart enough to avoid drugs and AIDS? Will they know how to handle differences without resorting to violence? Will they learn the survival skills needed to participate effectively in our society?

The type of intelligence required to handle this latter set of questions isn't acquired by memorizing rules and regulations, or through the use of technology. These challenges call for the development of students' social and emotional intelligence, along with their academic abilities. Emotionally healthy young people learn how to earn respect, establish a sense of belonging in a valued group, and build a sense of personal worth based on mastery of useful skills, including social skills. According to the Carnegie Council on Adolescent Development (*Turning Points*, 1989), "finding ways for adults and students to develop personalized relationships in schools is crucial" (p. 16). Nevertheless, rarely does a school program of studies include helping students deal personally with the social and emotional problems they (like all of us) must confront.

Recent research studies such as those conducted by George Vaillant (2000) have begun to document the connection between a child's emotional skills and future success in life. Schools that ignore emotional education, or believe "there is simply no time" for it, do so at the peril of the students in their charge. True, the demands on teachers and school systems are already great, even excessive. Nevertheless, more and more educators see emotional and social development as the foundation for their students' success—in school and life.

1

In his celebrated book, *Emotional Intelligence: Why It Can Matter More Than IQ*, science writer Daniel Goleman (1995) argues that qualities such as self-control, motivation, and empathy are the "master aptitudes" that determine how well human beings use their intellect. A school that deliberately, collectively addresses the development of these abilities helps its students acquire skills that every adult recognizes as the foundation for a satisfying life.

School programs that increase opportunities for student involvement through peer tutoring, school and community service, cooperative learning, and involvement with prosocial adults produce positive behavioral and academic results for students (Hawkins, 1997). At schools like Williamsburg Middle School and Yorktown High School (both in Arlington, Virginia), the Nueva Learning Center in California, and the New Haven Public School District in Connecticut, deliberate efforts promote the connection between a nurturing school climate, academic excellence, and the development of emotional and social intelligence. At each grade level, students learn or receive reinforcement in specific skills—from learning how to give and receive negative feedback to how to handle anger, for example—through engaging school activities like Big Brother/Big Sister and through classroom experiences like role-playing and cooperative learning.

In well-organized programs such as Big Brother/Big Sister, younger students have the opportunity to learn from older students, while the latter have the opportunity to learn (and care) about others through experience. Within the classroom, teachers can use the inevitable problems and situations that arise when students work in groups, to provide valuable SEL lessons to the whole class. These schoolwide and classroom learning experiences promote social and emotional learning in a practical, natural way that is more effective than simply imparting factual knowledge.

Integrating these types of educational experiences into a student's day and curriculum does not diminish an emphasis on academics or intellectual achievement. By helping students grow in their awareness of themselves and others, their emotions and how to handle them, we are helping them achieve academically as well. Who cannot recall being so disturbed in school by something that maturity revealed as quite trivial, that nevertheless prevented real learning from taking place at the time? Addressing the "inner lives" of students, and their interpersonal skills, acknowledges the fundamental importance of these dimensions of life, beyond those occasions when a troubled young person may seek a professional's help.

The curriculum of American education has long been largely externally oriented, and therefore attention to the inner life is viewed with some suspicion. In an educational climate that often focuses solely on standardized test results, others remain wary of learning opportunities that do more than require the mastery of externalized bodies of knowledge, through memorization or textbook analysis. Understanding self? Understanding others? Some would assert that there's just no time for "teaching" this in school, beyond the health class perhaps, or the guidance office when a specific problem arises.

Certainly, students have been required in the past to write or speak from the heart. These occasions often have produced some memorable statements within the classrooms of experienced teachers, but such work usually has been relegated to a special assignment in a particular subject, understood to be a "detour" from the "more important" requirements of the curriculum. The different kind of knowledge, or intelligence, required to address such an assignment has not been promoted or rewarded in most schools, especially those offering "college-prep" programs. Again, the conventional wisdom has been that there's really not enough time.

Proponents of school programs in social and emotional education are not advocating substituting emotional or interpersonal learning for academics. They are recognizing, however, that in order to live an integrated, balanced life, some self-understanding, self-control, and interpersonal skills are needed. Otherwise, all the academic instruction in the world may never have the opportunity to take root and flourish.

Social/emotional education *and* academic instruction—we need both. As educators, we simply cannot abandon our responsibility to address each young person's life as an integrated whole. Surely, this is a daunting challenge, but one worth pursuing. Educators are still discovering the best ways to do this; this book offers some ideas and suggestions that have met with some success. At the same time, every thoughtful and experienced educator could no doubt add other dimensions to what is offered here. The needs and goals of each school, faculty, and student body are unique, and no two programs will likely share identical designs. The important thing is that educators incorporate the social and emotional dimension into the educational programs of every school.

SOME EXAMPLES: BEGINNINGS

Yorktown, a public high school with grades 9–12, is located in Arlington, Virginia, just south of Washington, DC. With over 1,550 students, it prides itself on meeting the needs of a diverse population, in which 40% belong to minority groups, and over 25% have a first-language background other than English. A recent ranking of high schools in the Washington metropolitan area compiled by the *Washington Post* placed Yorktown in the top 10 most challenging academic schools in the area.

Prior to becoming principal of Yorktown in 1997, I had developed the conviction that a strong academic program alone did not constitute a truly excellent school. After a short while, it became clear to me that the faculty, staff, parents, and even many students also held that conviction. I am proud that Yorktown works every day at offering a first-rate academic curriculum to its students, along with a strong, developing social and emotional program.

After a full year of planning, preparation, and evaluation, the faculty and students at Yorktown designed their own initiative for implementing SEL in the classroom and school at large. Soon after, Williamsburg Middle School, the largest feeder school to the high school, also decided to create its own program. Margaret McCourt-Dirner, principal at Williamsburg, explains: "We are also committed to the idea of addressing social and emotional skills and attitudes with the same industry that we address academic ones. We are talking about skills these students desperately need, such as how to communicate, problem-solve, and work together in community. Some students need to be reminded of the importance of self-discipline and self-control; at the very least, we are raising their awareness."

Well-planned SEL programs have been well received by students and teachers, including those initially resistant to the idea. Even limited initiatives that deal with social and emotional domains have shown progress in improving students' abilities to handle transition and in increasing their prosocial behavior. When students of any age learn to control their emotions, the chances increase that thought will precede action in the classroom setting and outside the school as well. Finally, in a society where the importance of appreciating diversity, multiculturalism, and equity must be underscored, these students also learn to value differences and demonstrate increased sensitivity to the feelings of others.

When a school community decides to design and implement an explicit, schoolwide program in social and emotional education, it is asserting its belief in a broad definition of intelligence and success and its commitment to helping students develop their capacity to make intelligent decisions and develop healthy interpersonal relationships. A key advantage to this type of initiative is that it targets *all* students, and is potentially beneficial to everyone in the total school community.

At Yorktown High School, several students returned from a summer workshop at another high school impressed with some behavioral reminders creatively publicized throughout the building. Convinced something similar could have a positive impact at Yorktown, they persuaded the Student Life Committee to design and create "10 Principles of Success," which no visitor or student to the school can possibly miss. Response to the initiative has been positive: Students and faculty report that the messages serve as helpful reinforcers of desirable attitudes and behaviors that promote success.

Just a year later, a committee of students and faculty completed "Goals of Community Behavior," designed to articulate the kind of environment in which students want to learn and faculty want to work. Throughout the school, the colorful, student-designed "Yorktown ROCS" posters (Figure 1.1) serve as a reminder to the school community of the importance of respecting others, the community, and self. Bookmarks, a smaller version of the poster, are mailed home to parents and distributed to students after a short television broadcast on an SEL theme, and they work as another practical symbol.

At Williamsburg Middle School, the week before school begins, seventh-grade students provide opportunities for personalized tours of the school for incoming sixth-grade students. Prior to that orientation, they meet with the principal to talk about the importance of understanding the fears and concerns incoming students may have. Providing such an opportunity for students is more likely to promote the generalization of respect for others than would a lecture on the topic from an administrator or a teacher.

Social and emotional education can be provided in a variety of ways within the school setting. Some schools provide it as a distinct course; others include it as part of a health or guidance unit. Still others develop their own set of basic social and emotional skills that they want to promote in their students (through consultation with teachers, parents, and the students themselves), and then design a plan for promoting those skills in an organized, comprehensive fashion.

At the Nueva Learning Center in California, a comprehensive program designed to help students understand their own feelings, and those that arise in relationships, is taught in the "Self Science" curriculum. In the New Haven, Connecticut, schools, the "Social Competence Program" helps students deal with conflicts through classroom and playground efforts, along with student and parent education programs. Here, peer mediation is taught at school and also explained to parents. Such initiatives represent just two of the numerous school-based programs that involve the promotion and development of social and emotional learning.

In the end, the responsibility for teaching students how to deal with their social and emotional lives cannot be reserved solely to their families or strictly to the guidance and health departments of schools. All the professionals in the school have a responsibility for teaching young people that their minds must work with their hearts if they hope to live successful and fulfilled lives.

STRATEGIES FOR SUCCESS

1. *Develop a comprehensive plan.*

The promotion of SEL along with a strong academic program comes about because a school administration and faculty decide to expand the definition

Figure 1.1. Goals of Community Behavior at Yorktown High School, Arlington, Virginia

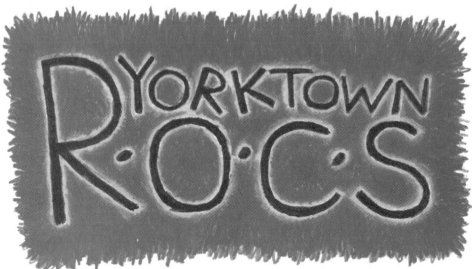

Respect: Others, Your Community, and most of all, Your Self!

Respect for Others:
Acceptance of individual differences
Appreciation of diversity
Mutual concern for others

Respect for Community:
Consideration for personal, school, and neighborhood property
Emphasis on being a positive representative of Yorktown
Maintenance of a healthy and productive school environment

Respect for Self:
Development of one's full potential
Involvement in extracurricular activities
Ability to seek support from staff and other students when needed
Promotion of high self-esteem

These goals were written by students within the Yorktown community in an effort to encourage and promote mutual respect for one another.

of intelligence and success to include social and emotional skills and attitudes. These are educators who do not want students to graduate believing they are successful simply because they have achieved high grades or superior test scores. In addition, they want to recognize other examples of intelligence seen in students of all levels of academic ability, such as the capacity to get along with a wide range of peers, or to diffuse potentially hostile situations, or to show empathy for others in need. In brief, they most often have made a conscious decision to provide their students not only with knowledge and facts, but also with other important skills that will help them in school and life itself.

An important point from the start: Administrators and faculty can design and implement a practical program, suited to their particular school's needs, without turning the existing daily schedule upside down. In addition, while ideally all teachers should be involved to some degree, an effective program can allow for varied levels of faculty involvement, depending on individual preferences and existing responsibilities. With that in mind, these guidelines may provide assistance as you think about how your school might develop and implement an SEL program.

Social and emotional education experts agree that students are more likely to develop these skills when they are promoted in all aspects of school life. Furthermore, a school is more likely to enhance its overall learning climate when it adopts a comprehensive strategy. The most effective approach infuses social and emotional education into all academic disciplines, along with specific schoolwide activities designed to provide experience in developing related skills. As part of this, many schools provide a variety of service opportunities as just one aspect of their total effort to help students develop responsibility, self-awareness, interpersonal skills, and empathy toward others.

2. Include modeling by school personnel as part of your mission.

Caring is best promoted by example.

Perhaps the most important ingredient in any successful program is an appreciation by every administrator, faculty member, and coach that their own skill in handling emotions, and in developing positive relationships with students and colleagues, is among the most powerful methods of helping to educate students who will then want to possess these same abilities.

3. Get everyone on board.

Another crucial element of an effective, explicit social and emotional education program is a commitment by administrators and faculty to the concept that such a program is an indispensable part of the school's mission. For a program to be successful, there must be a sense of ownership among teachers, students, and families, and time must be provided for staff to reflect and plan along the way. Indeed, it is in the interests of students, teachers, parents, and the community at large that social and emotional learning receive the same thought and creativity we associate with any effective academic program. These attitudes go a long way toward ensuring the development of a more positive, caring school community and an enhanced learning environment for all.

SOME BENEFITS TO KEEP IN MIND

Initially, parents and educators may resist the idea of adding yet another content area to the curriculum, believing it will detract from children's academic education. However, it can actually enhance their ability to achieve. Research increasingly supports that academic instruction alone does not assist students in developing into responsible, caring, and academically competent learners (Payton et al., 2000). Like most adults, young people learn best when they have the tools to address other issues going on in their lives, and see the connection between their academic work and real life. Programs that explicitly seek to increase opportunities for young people to be actively involved in helping others within the school and in the community, and to increase the occasions when they learn cooperatively in the classroom, produce positive behavioral and academic results. When an entire faculty focuses on such efforts, the learning environment in the school is enhanced.

Another important benefit of organized programs is the common language they provide administrators and faculty for working toward these goals together, each aware of what the other is doing. Individual teachers who have always attempted to help students address some of these concerns through their own teaching now have the explicit support of the efforts of others throughout the school.

Consider how your school already addresses issues related to emotional and interpersonal development, and how it might benefit from a schoolwide effort to educate students in these domains. Ask yourself what the benefits of such an effort might be for *all* concerned, and whether the potential benefits for students who have had exposure to such a program outweigh the inevitable difficulties involved in establishing something "new." How can you build on everything your school presently offers its students in order to expand their understanding that intelligence is not solely a set of cognitive skills?

Finally, as parents and educators, we recognize the many changes in our society over the past 50 years, and our obligation to continue seeking new answers to long-standing questions. How do we help our students achieve their potential in every area of life? How do we enable them to achieve academically, and at the same time teach them to manage their emotions and relationships with intelligence? In today's world, these two are inextricably linked.

This book does not provide a ready-made program for duplication. It does present ideas and strategies to help schools begin to consider, design, and develop a program in social and emotional education. Once again, each school must address its own unique issues, needs, and resources in order to get a program in social and emotional education off the ground.

While designing programs in SEL requires tackling something relatively new, the potential rewards of doing so for students, faculty, and the school at large become apparent over time. Accept my best wishes as you begin or continue the important adventure of designing a program meant to meet the needs of students in the changing and challenging society in which we live.

2 Designing a Program: The Basic Principles

What are the ideas and principles that form the foundation of strong programs in social and emotional learning?

Perhaps the most significant principle underlying a comprehensive approach is the importance of fostering school communities where social and emotional learning is modeled, deliberately taught, and affirmed. Young people are quick to observe incongruities between words and actions; as teachers and administrators, we cannot teach young people to control their emotions if we lose our patience with them at every turn.

GETTING READY

While there is no single, effective approach to social and emotional education in a school, there are some basic principles that one should bear in mind from the start when planning an organized, comprehensive effort to address SEL issues.

1. *Social and emotional learning promotes intelligent decision-making as the basis of healthy, positive behavior.*

   A school committed to social and emotional learning for all its students states and promotes its belief in the importance of self-respect and respect for others, the importance in daily life of thinking before acting, and the fact that there are effective and ineffective ways of dealing with and working with others.

   Such a school discusses issues related to these areas, promotes them in varied ways within the school, defines them in terms of behavior that can be observed in the life of the school and outside the school, and has staff members who are committed to developing their own social and emotional learning.

   In a school committed to promoting social and emotional learning, student success is not measured by academic success alone. Truly successful graduates from such a school have learned to appreciate their own value and to respect the value of others. For these reasons, they are more inclined to think before responding to others than to respond in an impulsive or violent fashion.

2. *Social and emotional education must provide students with experiences that show the link between thinking, feeling, and behavior.*

For social and emotional education to be effective, students must be taught explicitly that how they think affects how they feel—and that how they feel can affect how they behave, so that they must learn to be aware of and control their emotions. Bullies can learn that instead of striking out violently against another, it is possible to think of other, more peaceful options and respond accordingly. Children who lack confidence can learn the connection between what they are saying to themselves and how that affects the way they feel.

3. *Effective social and emotional education programs incorporate direct and indirect instruction into all areas of school life.*

An effective SEL program will be as comprehensive as possible, multiyear, and multicomponent (Zins, Elias, Greenberg, & Weissberg, 2000).

A thoughtful, deliberate approach to social and emotional education programs includes deliberate ways to educate students in this domain, and no area is left unaffected.

- Faculty and staff understand the importance of modeling and providing examples
- Expectations regarding students' interactions with each other (and staff) are made clear, and explicit disrespectful behavior is not ignored
- Athletic coaches and moderators of extracurricular activities appreciate the school's SEL emphasis and recognize they must conduct themselves with students accordingly; students are expected to interact with each other in after-school activities with the same degree of respect they are challenged to bring to interactions during the school day
- SEL principles are integrated into lessons across disciplines, in explicit and informal ways
- Schoolwide initiatives, such as theme-based assemblies, reinforce SEL principles
- Awards and honors include recognition of students who demonstrate outstanding SEL skills and attitudes

A comprehensive approach such as this endeavors to infuse social and emotional learning into all components of school life.

4. *For an SEL program to be effective and take root, the school's and each classroom's climate must be characterized by caring and respect.*

High expectations for both academic achievement and behavior must start with the adults in the building and be promoted among the students in their charge. Signs of a lack of respect or tolerance for others are not ignored but addressed—among administrators, faculty, staff, and students—in schools that have established social and emotional literacy as a central piece of their educational mission.

5. *To promote social and emotional learning, students need opportunities to problem-solve with others and to examine what worked and did not work in those interactions and collaborations.*

To develop their self-knowledge and capacity to deal effectively with others, students need a range of opportunities to apply decision-making and problem-solving skills to various situations. The educational goal becomes more than the end product, final presentation, or project; it includes an examination of how the student (and her peers) worked together. What behaviors and attitudes helped the group; which hindered? What are the characteristics of effective and ineffective collaborators in group situations? What are the strengths each person brings to a cooperative learning project? Through varied experiences, students can develop the skills and habits that will help them beyond school and throughout life.

6. *Effective social and emotional education enhances a challenging academic program and promotes higher academic expectations for all.*

Students are more likely to achieve in a school and classroom climate characterized by mutual respect and caring. They sense when they are valued as individuals with diverse personalities, needs, and abilities; for this reason, a school staff has a particular role in promoting high behavioral expectations for students (and for the staff itself). Academic learning and social/emotional education are interconnected and mutually supportive.

7. *A school committed to SEL must consider ways to involve parents in its social and emotional learning efforts.*

No school program, no matter how creative and comprehensive, can take the place of the social and emotional education a young person receives at home. The school must take every opportunity to share with parents its goals in the area of social and emotional education. Parents should be invited to participate, and even to provide leadership when possible. Clearly, success in all areas of a student's education is enhanced when family and school work together—this is particularly true in the social and emotional domains.

8. *The fact that evaluation of program success in the social/emotional area is less quantifiable than academic achievement should not be a deterrent to initiating a program.*

While effective social and emotional education must include an effort to assess progress among individual students and the school as a whole, it is more difficult to assess progress in this area than it is to tabulate standardized test score results. This should never be a reason to avoid program implementation. School surveys, student behavioral reports, and staff questionnaires can all be used as aids to assess progress. Objective evaluations tracking students before and after they are exposed to a course or program, or comparing students who are exposed to such experiences with those who are not, will help glean concrete data to support what should be observable: improvement in the school climate and the social competence of students involved.

9. *No single course or program will answer every student problem.*

Progress takes time; success must be viewed in the long term. It takes each of us many years to become the person we are today, and many years to change. The same is true of our students. Ideally, students receive education in these important domains at home from the time they are young children; during their developing years, the most fortunate receive it at home and in school. To maximize effectiveness, lessons need to be designed to meet the developmental needs of the child or adolescent, and repeated at different ages in different ways.

10. *When starting the SEL program, assure faculty that staff development opportunities in this area will be built into each year's professional development program.*

Even more than professional development opportunities, experienced teachers need and deserve to hear that they, better than anyone else, have the ability to bring SEL instruction to life in the classroom. In my experience, competent teachers quickly catch on to what constitutes effective SEL lessons, and most enjoy the challenge of creating them.

Nevertheless, professional development reinforces teacher success, provides opportunities for the exchange of ideas, and enriches knowledge of theory and practice. The SEL programs that last the longest tend to be the most effective. Staff development will help sustain the interest and enthusiasm of those involved in the challenge of delivering SEL instruction.

DESIGNING A PROGRAM

Before beginning the specifics of program design, the individual interested in initiating the project should have some understanding of the following:

- How social and emotional learning fosters the goals of the school system and the particular school where the program will be implemented
- The student outcomes that will result from the institution of a social/emotional learning program (i.e., increased self-awareness and self-motivation, improved interpersonal skills and ability to make good decisions, etc.)
- What it means to develop a school community that is committed to teaching children to be respectful and caring young people
- In what ways the overall school climate will be enhanced, and how that also will be advantageous to the local school community and its citizens

An effective means for implementing and evaluating SEL programs is the establishment of a steering committee, with a chair or two co-chairs to coordinate efforts. While the ideal committee will include one teacher from every discipline and/or grade level (depending on the number of staff within a school), the most important factor is the genuine interest of each participant in SEL development. At least one school administrator should serve on the committee.

The steering committee's considerations should include the following issues:

- Identification of student needs and initiatives already in place
- Implementation plans designed to meet student needs while avoiding duplication of existing programs
- Coordination and planning of ongoing professional development for teachers
- Identification of specific responsibilities for faculty, support personnel, and parents
- Allocation of adequate time and resources for those responsible for program delivery
- Impact of program development on students, faculty, and overall school climate

Members of the steering committee should ensure that they provide progress reports to faculty throughout the year. What is taking place in the school? What schoolwide initiatives have taken place? Teachers who have presented successful lessons should be invited to share what worked, or did not, with their colleagues. These efforts at ongoing communication help maintain interest in and support for SEL programs.

Single Course or Curriculum Infusion?

A fundamental, important decision must be made from the start: Will the school provide social and emotional education across academic disciplines and through special activities *or* will it delegate that responsibility to the curriculum of an individual course, such as health or the guidance program?

A separate course has the advantage of shifting the educational responsibility in this domain to a specific teacher, in a particular year, with a clearly delineated curriculum. While this is more easily implemented than a more comprehensive approach, it does less to help all students and teachers, providing a Band-Aid solution for a problem that requires much more.

Infusing social and emotional learning across the curriculum, on the other hand, reinforces and enhances each academic discipline and is less likely to be eliminated from a school's course of studies during times of budget constraint. This book is geared to those schools and districts that decide to take this latter "infusion" approach, with the addition of specific schoolwide activities.

Perhaps the most practical advice that can be offered is to investigate existing quality programs and then *tailor* them to meet your school's particular situation and desired outcomes. For example, an American school abroad may need to design a component to help students deal with the feeling of isolation that can come with moving to a foreign country; another school may have to address entirely different needs. Do significant issues stand out with a particular grade: lack of self-discipline, inability to listen or follow directions, lack of tolerance across groups, reluctance to assume leadership? Meetings with staff by grade level can yield insights into a particular class, which can later help shape a program.

Goals and Objectives

When considering establishing a program to foster social and emotional learning, remember that one goal is to enhance academic learning *and* all that is being done in the school already. Like a map, the design of such a program can provide guidance as to where you are, where you might like to be, and how you intend to get there. No one blueprint can ensure effective program planning or design. Your particular school, its student population, and its unique needs will give important signs as to the kind of program best suited for your school, with its particular staff and students.

The general goals and objectives of a school's program should include, but not be limited to, the following:

1. *To foster a positive, caring, and respectful climate within each classroom and the school at large.*

How is discipline handled in each teacher's classroom and by the administrators? The role of appropriate punishment in a school need not change. At the same time, designing or including an educational component to disciplinary policies can require students to slow down and think about what they did and what led up to a problematic incident in the first place. Whenever possible, it is helpful to have students write down what they were thinking and feeling before they acted and then indicate how they would handle a similar situation more constructively in the future.

2. *To promote, where possible and practical, specific themes and skills of social and emotional development—as agreed upon by the faculty and administration—within each grade level.*

At LaSalle Academy, each grade level has a specific SEL focus, tied into the perceived needs of students and their developmental level (e.g., grade 9—respect for self, grade 10—understanding others, grade 11—leadership, grade 12—service). Throughout each year, decision-making forms the foundation for each of these themes (see Association for Supervision and Curriculum Development, 1997).

3. *To teach, model, and encourage the development of social and emotional competencies while conducting extracurricular activities.*

Schools must do whatever possible to ensure that the message and experiences students receive *during* the school day are similar to what they receive in athletics and extracurricular programs. For this reason, part-time coaches and activity moderators also must understand, agree to, and be held accountable for promoting the fundamental messages of social and emotional learning.

4. *To provide specific schoolwide programs, as practical and appropriate, that help meet the social and emotional education goals set by the school community.*

These goals generally are reflected in the school mission statement or the goals of the district in which the school is located. Such programs explicitly promote a caring school environment, providing opportunities for an "inner" education while individual students reach out to others. Programs like Peer Mediation, Big Brother/Big Sister, Community Service, and the like offer as many important experiences to the leader as they do to the person targeted by the outreach program.

5. *To provide a more comprehensive approach for helping students develop their self-awareness, interpersonal, and problem-solving skills than a superficial, Band-Aid approach would permit.*

This schoolwide approach utilizes every avenue of communication: classroom lessons, schoolwide programs, theme-based assemblies, and the manner in which students are dealt with during and after school. Time is taken regularly, inside and outside the classroom, to have students consider the ways they and others make decisions and solve problems. This requires the commitment of all staff to this important component of a young person's education, and the regular, deliberate articulation of its importance by school administrators and program coordinator(s).

STARTING AT THE END: PROGRAM EVALUATION

We live during a time when the effectiveness of schools is increasingly measured by students' scores on standardized tests. Since the effectiveness of SEL programs is not as easily measured by pen and paper examinations, evaluation presents one of the larger challenges facing a school seeking to implement such an initiative. What evidence do you have that your program works?

Since the goal of an SEL program is to meet student needs in a practical way, planning the components of program implementation naturally takes priority initially. At a point when specifics have begun to take shape, however, the assistance of a researcher can prove most helpful in designing a sound evaluation instrument. Very often, schools think about program evaluation only after implementation is complete, creating some difficulties that otherwise might have been avoided.

Before evaluating the program, you should identify what it has been designed to target or treat. What exactly are the problems the classroom and schoolwide strategies have been designed to address? What are the primary goals of the program? The purpose of the program must be clearly understood and articulated before the first year of implementation. The goals should be expressed as tangible, clearly stated outcomes and should include both short-term and long-term goals.

An effective schoolwide program in social and emotional education should have a discernible impact on school climate, student (and faculty) awareness, and ultimately student behavior. In designing a plan for the evaluation of a school program in social and emotional education, you should keep the following in mind:

- How will you know whether the program has been implemented as the steering committee planned?
- How will you know whether the schoolwide and classroom components are both in place?
- When and how will you measure the results of both dimensions of the program?
- Will individual students have an opportunity to provide feedback? Midyear or at the end of the year?

- When and how will teachers and administrators have the opportunity to offer their perceptions of the program's effectiveness?
- How will parents' concerns, questions, and suggestions be addressed?
- What aspects of the program should remain in place, be revised, or deleted in the future?

In the same way that a steering committee plans the components of the SEL program, it can be helpful to establish an evaluation team that will design the questions that need to be answered and determine other specifics regarding the evaluation process. The practitioners involved in teaching and implementing a program often do not have the time to design and implement an evaluation instrument as well.

A word of caution: Social and emotional problems have a variety of causes, and no single program can address them all. You need to ensure that goals are practical, attainable, and measurable. In researching the effectiveness of prevention programs, studies by the W. T. Grant Foundation (Hawkins, Catalano, et al., 1992) and others show that well-designed, competency-based programs are more effective than single-shot assemblies designed to target a particular problem (e.g., substance abuse).

The primary purpose of the evaluation process is to assure the continued growth and improvement of the SEL program.

- One individual, familiar with the program's purpose and design, should be designated to coordinate the evaluation and to head a team that will evaluate the program as it evolves.
- When designing the program, the steering committee should establish a mechanism for ongoing assessment during at least the first 3 years of the program.
- One aspect of program evaluation that should be included is professional development—what training will be most cost effective in establishing and maintaining the program?
- Flexibility should be built into any assessment. By their nature, programs in social and emotional education promote skills that are not as easily measured as a student's mathematics ability. An evaluation program must be flexible enough to be sensitive to that fundamental difference.
- The evaluation process should include opportunities for feedback from students, parents, and faculty. Social and emotional education means something different to each group, and each constituency views such a program from a different perspective.
- Recognizing that virtually all schools have a variety of programs in place, before establishing a specific SEL initiative it is valuable to evaluate the impact it will have on other, pre-existing programs. Are all efforts in this domain coordinated to increase effectiveness and avoid unnecessary duplication of initiatives?

3 Schools as Challenging, Caring Communities

Every school needs a unifying purpose or mission, something that serves as a universally understood "bottom line" that inspires faculty and serves students.

Whatever that common purpose, an explicit recognition of the social and emotional dimension of school life helps provide a foundation upon which other achievements can be built and provides a clear signal about what type of climate the school wants to create. Emphasizing that dimension lets the school community know that whatever its academic goals may be, they will be accomplished in a supportive, respectful environment characterized by interest in every individual.

As educators, we are remiss if we do not try to provide students with a positive social and emotional environment within which they can develop academically and personally. This requires that the school and individual classroom spaces be made as inviting and warm as practical. Wherever possible, administrators and teachers in schools that have such an environment focus on individual students and needs rather than on "groups" of students.

Within the classrooms, experienced teachers understand the crucial role of thoughtful, proactive classroom management. When students work with their teachers (and administrators) to develop classroom contracts and guidelines for student behavior, negative and disruptive factors are decreased. Such contracts implicitly emphasize the expectation that students will practice self-management skills, and encourage them to think, monitor, and evaluate their own behavior. When the school and classrooms foster both personal growth and academic learning, even students with less support outside the school have some opportunity to have their lives enriched by a nurturing environment during the school day.

The literature reveals that when schools become nurturing, caring places, key characteristics become evident.

- Students feel a sense of self-worth and acceptance
- Students feel safe and involved in their education
- Mutual trust and positive interactions occur between teachers and students

- A sense of community, family, and collaboration exists in the school
- Everyone values individual differences, and each person is respected and nurtured
- There is a sense of caring among individuals and a collective sense of responsibility for student success
- The need for self-actualization is respected
- There is recognition of a wide range of talents and the need for empowering all individuals
- Teachers have an in-depth knowledge of students
- The school models the values of the community and involves the community in the education of its students
- Teachers model caring attitudes for students
- Teachers demonstrate a love for their subject matter and continuously search for competence
- Students value themselves and others (Green, 1997)

To foster maximum student achievement, and to promote the total growth of students, school leaders must deliberately create the kind of community in which adults and students *want* to work and learn. This is not easy, but ultimately it helps increase the creativity and effectiveness of faculty and students alike.

One reason for establishing SEL programs within the school is to help create and perpetuate this type of positive, caring school climate—one that supports students (and staff) while it challenges them to reach beyond their grasp.

SCHOOL LEADERS: SHAPING THE ENVIRONMENT

The creation of any school climate starts with the school leaders. Their principles and beliefs provide the foundation for the school's common purpose. The way they interact with others sends the most powerful message of the type of atmosphere they want to establish. It is up to all the school leaders— principals, teachers, support staff, student leaders, and even parents—to help create and maintain a strong, positive, challenging, and caring school environment. Without such a climate, faculty morale will suffer, student achievement may not realize its full potential, and other school initiatives will likely enjoy only short-lived success.

Regrettably, some schools, over time, develop a distinctly negative school climate—characterized more by apathy and fragmentation than by hopefulness and caring. In such a school, the focus generally has shifted from serving students to accommodating adults, and new ideas are routinely met with cynicism or attack.

No one wants to work or learn in this type of school. Schools with strong, positive climates are characterized by a palpable ethos of caring and concern, a shared understanding of the need for high expectations for *all*, and a recognition that faculty, staff, and administrators have one fundamental goal: helping students learn.

When all members of the school staff are committed to this vision of the school community, each individual can recognize his role in a larger purpose. A teacher need no longer feel his efforts are isolated or fragmented, but part of something greater than his classroom alone. A faculty committed to promoting a challenging academic and positive social/emotional environment, is more likely to send consistent (rather than conflicting) messages to its students.

Ensuring Safety: A Fundamental Need

If students (or staff) do not feel safe, it is difficult for the school to have a positive impact on their lives. While safety issues must be confronted directly, a school leader also must consider how safety can be ensured while maintaining or developing a positive, nurturing environment. A key component of student safety centers on how inclined students feel to trust and speak with at least one significant adult in the building. If the school takes on the atmosphere of an "armed camp," it becomes less likely that this type of relationship can develop.

When planning to ensure the safety of the total school environment, you should consider the following:

- As school leader, do you encourage your faculty and staff to recognize and face problems that exist within the school, rather than denying, justifying, or rationalizing them? Have you been clear about the action(s) you want staff to take when they observe a student violation of a school rule; are consequences clear to students?
- What means can be taken to prevent problems before they occur or to resolve them promptly? The answer could include security cameras, but it also might include new student-led activities such as Peer Mediation and Diversity Peer Leadership.
- Are security personnel aware of a school philosophy that promotes respect for all? In their daily supervisory role, do they respect students (and fellow staff)? Do they have the interpersonal skills required to help students follow school rules without unnecessarily escalating the tension of a situation? The safety of all is compromised whenever students begin to feel they are learning in a "them" versus "us" environment.

- To the extent possible, are faculty schedules and room assignments designed to permit teachers to be in the halls outside their classrooms at the start and end of the day, as well as between class periods? This practice also makes it easier for students to know where they are likely to locate a particular teacher when a special need arises.
- Do the principal, administrators, faculty, and students collaborate whenever possible in an effort to solve problems? Is communication among these groups frequent and clear? Are school regulations unambiguous and enforced equally among all groups and individuals? Do administrators and faculty have high behavioral and academic expectations for *all* students?
- When a disturbing incident occurs in the school, does the principal make it a practice to keep faculty informed of the facts in a timely fashion? Does the principal make it a point to thank those members of the faculty and staff who do an especially conscientious job with supervision, especially after a violent disturbance or tragedy?
- Whenever a large group of students is scheduled to attend an event, such as a schoolwide assembly, are expectations for student behavior and teacher supervision—prior to, during, and at the conclusion of the event—clear and unambiguous?

LAYING THE GROUNDWORK

As a principal or other school leader, you should take time at the start of the year to consider the following:

- What are some of the key components of a caring, challenging community?
- Given your unique responsibilities within the school, what does it mean to you to be a community builder?
- How does the way you see yourself as a community builder influence your vision for the school? How does it affect the strategies you use to achieve your goals and responsibilities? How does it affect the actions that you take?

These questions, first considered by a smaller group of school leaders but eventually discussed by a broad range of faculty and staff, provide the groundwork for individuals to take ownership of the school. One helpful activity is to ask faculty and staff to express in writing how they understand their role in establishing the kind of climate we have been discussing. Individually or as a group, everyone working at the school might take time to write a response to the following prompts:

- Create a personal statement that reflects your commitment to help build a challenging, caring school community.
- Consistent with that statement, describe three specific actions you intend to take to build your school into a caring community.

Depending on the level of trust within the building, these decisions can be either shared with others or placed in a sealed envelope and returned to each person later in the school year. At that point, faculty members can examine how faithful they have been in following through on their personal statements and three actions.

BUILDING THE FOUNDATION FOR CARING

When trying to shape the school climate into one that is challenging and caring, a principal and other school leaders can engage in specific behaviors.

- Explicitly state behavioral expectations to students, faculty, and staff, and reinforce these throughout the year.
- Encourage staff and faculty to *not* ignore student behaviors of which they disapprove; inform students from the start that at this school all faculty feel a responsibility for all students. (Students should not be surprised, therefore, if they are held accountable for their behavior by a faculty member they do not know.)
- Communicate core values, such as the importance of mutual respect and valuing diversity, in word and action.
- Use student successes as an opportunity to celebrate not only the student(s), but also the faculty member(s) who helped the student(s) achieve success.
- Design creative means for highlighting and publicizing the many good things that happen in most schools each day.
- Create a collaborative problem-solving approach, where faculty, staff, students, and administrators work together to reach solutions; avoid a them versus us approach to school management.
- Behave in such a way that it becomes clear that the mission of the school is to help *every* student achieve success and that the goal of nonteaching staff (including administrators) is to help teachers meet the learning needs of students.

School leaders who are effective in creating a positive, challenging, caring school climate are clear in their expectations for teacher behavior within the classroom. Specifically, such leaders clearly articulate an expectation that teachers will challenge and engage *every* student, encouraging rather than discouraging them along the way. Mutual respect is the bottom line not only in the school at large, but in each classroom as well.

Clear expectations for students and consistent treatment of all students communicate respect and demonstrate an interest in the students themselves, as well as in the subjects they are learning. Adults dealing with students understand the expectation that they will interact with students in a way that creates a nurturing, caring climate where students feel challenged yet supported. At times, this requires taking the time to teach students the skills of cooperation and conflict resolution; it *always* requires modeling by the teacher who articulates clear student expectations and who genuinely cares about the success and welfare of every student in the room.

ROLE OF THE PRINCIPAL

The principal's role in developing a caring and challenging community is crucial, demanding leadership by word and action. Among the responsibilities the principal must juggle are: moving the institution forward, promoting high student achievement, accepting responsibility for all students and staff, and leading the development of a school climate that contributes to effective teaching and learning. In relation to the latter, the elements that determine success are as varied as the interactions among faculty, staff, and students and include the quality of the school facility. More than one single item, it is a combination of factors that determines the quality of the overall learning environment. As an administrator, you should try asking yourself the following questions:

1. *Have you paid attention to the physical environment of the school, inside and outside?* Do you seek the assistance of students, parents, and faculty/staff? How would they suggest making the school more attractive and inviting?
2. *What efforts can be made within your school to create an environment that supports the healthy social development of young people?* Are there locations and opportunities within the school for students to have positive social involvement with peers and adults? If social and emotional education is to be effective, it must be supported by the overall environment in which children learn (Elias et al., 1997).
3. *Have you helped faculty and staff develop a shared sense of purpose?* Are the mission and goals of the school clear?
4. *Do you encourage collaborative participation* and consult a wide range of constituent groups before making important decisions?
5. *Do you seek opportunities to celebrate student accomplishments* and to publicly congratulate teachers who have been innovative in their approach to instruction?

6. *When you speak, do you look for opportunities to praise more than blame*, to encourage more than control? Is the fact that you care about the people in the school, students and staff alike, obvious from your words and actions?

7. During the final months of the school year, *do you seek written, candid feedback on important dimensions of school life from faculty, parents, and students?*

8. *Do you use that information with colleagues* to prepare for a more effective school year in the future, and communicate to the various groups that you have read and understood their concerns and suggestions?

Hiring and Supervision

The school climate a principal hopes to foster has an impact on one of her key responsibilities—hiring. Two components become important in selecting the best candidates for positions within the school: their professional competence, and their ability and willingness to promote a challenging and caring school environment. The latter is not always easy to judge, but responses to interview questions and letters of reference often provide clues to an individual's skills in working with colleagues and students, and the extent to which the individual feels responsible for *all* students. Ideally, teachers are effective instructors who are able to motivate, engage, and interact effectively with others when solving problems. When possible, it is desirable to hire teachers capable of integrating SEL with academic content. Once teachers have been hired, supervision and feedback should include both dimensions of performance. How do they perceive their role as teachers? Do they feel responsible for *all* learners and the entire school community? In the end, teachers are the key to creating the kind of classroom climate in which their students' SEL skills and attitudes are advanced.

Attitude and Professionalism

At a school that promotes SEL among students, the adults must understand that the way they treat students in their charge sets a powerful example. They use the problems and conflicts that arise to engage students in responses that are reflective, nonviolent, and creative. They treat students with interest, respect, courtesy, and kindness—and let students know that this is done deliberately and with effort. In so doing, they provide the kind of modeling that is more important than any individual lesson or activity.

SOLVING PROBLEMS

Difficulties arise between supervisors and staff for a variety of reasons, in all kinds of institutions, including schools. The norm, at times, is not to communicate with colleagues or subordinates directly and respectfully when there is a concern or problem. Some supervisors use sarcasm; others speak to colleagues but not to the individual with whom there is a problem; still others use silence or looks of disapproval. All of these behaviors foster an unhealthy emotional climate and have the effect over time of creating mistrust among faculty and staff toward the school administration. While it is challenging and often exhausting, school administrators—in particular, the principal—set a tone when in the face of problems they bring respectful candor to their dialogues with individual faculty members, staff, and students. Such forthright behavior fosters trust, promotes similar behavior in others, and enhances the emotional climate in which students learn and adults work.

MODELING FORGIVENESS

Of course, the principal is only human and will make errors in dealings with others. Most of us, at times, can be unintentionally rude or thoughtless, curt or insensitive. By modeling authenticity, and apologizing to individuals when the occasion warrants, the principal enhances his credibility as a leader and teacher.

If the school leadership encourages and practices a policy of respectful candor, it also must model an ability to forgive, forget, and proceed. An administrator who holds grudges or stops speaking with faculty or staff after a mistake has been made and addressed, communicates that mistakes will be neither forgiven nor forgotten. Especially when dealing with a well-meaning employee, it is important to communicate by word and example that one can remain a respected and productive staff member, even after making a mistake that necessitated direct and honest correction from, or discussion with, an administrator.

ENCOURAGING INVOLVEMENT

In many schools, there are faculty and staff who take an interest in their own domain (e.g., classroom), but do not bother to correct students when they see behavior of which they disapprove outside their own classroom or immediate area of responsibility. The principal must articulate from the start that one important expectation of faculty and staff is that they not ignore behavior anywhere in the school that is inappropriate, offensive, or in clear violation of rules. Support must then be given to those who do take the time and trouble to pursue such matters with students when they arise. The students themselves must understand from the start of the year that all faculty and staff are responsible for *all* students. This will limit the number of occasions in which they question why an adult they do not know corrects them.

If students, faculty, and staff understand this expectation, it can go a long way toward both enhancing the school climate and fostering an environment of mutual respect.

Fostering High Expectations

The need for care and compassion is obvious in today's climate. Along with those qualities, however, we must recognize the value of having high expectations—behaviorally and academically—for *all* students. A recent National Task Force Study on Minority Achievement commissioned by the College Board (1999) found that African-American students, as one example, frequently must deal with faculty—even well-meaning ones—who expect less of them. In a school that is characterized by social and emotional intelligence, the school leadership and faculty truly must themselves believe, and indoctrinate in all their students, the ethic that achievement and improvement are expected of all and are everyone's responsibility.

Celebrating Student Accomplishments

Consider your school. Which students receive praise? How and when do they receive recognition? Which students tend to *not* receive praise? How can occasions be designed to expand the student population that receives recognition? For example, if the students with the highest grade point averages generally are honored, how can this be expanded to also include those who have shown improvement? Are students who demonstrate special effort recognized? What low-profile clubs, activities, or organizations can be promoted and congratulated in ways ordinarily reserved for more popular activities? When and how are students who contribute positively to the school climate recognized for the special gifts they bring to the community?

Honing Communication Skills

Perhaps one of the greatest contributions the principal and other administrative leaders can bring to the emotional health of the school community is their commitment to evaluating and improving their own communication skills. The purpose of the exercise in Figure 3.1 is to help varied groups of school personnel, starting with the administration, identify and discuss communication challenges that need to be addressed individually or as a group. An exercise such as this, used periodically, can help the adults in the school work more effectively together. This increased effectiveness helps promote the type of positive climate in which SEL initiatives with students truly can flourish.

FIGURE 3.1. Communication Exercise

1. What particular "challenges" to communicating do we observe within the school?

    _____ Lack of focus or direction

    _____ Frenetic, impatient behavior

    _____ Too busy with "X" to care

    _____ Negative attitudes

    _____ Reaction more than proaction

    _____ Secretiveness about decisions

    _____ Judgmental attitudes

    _____ Indirect or unclear communication

    _____ Intolerance for mistakes

    _____ Frequent "closed-door" conversations

2. Consider how you participate in the above:

    What I do that does not make sense _____

    If I were brave, I would stop doing _____

    I question the effectiveness of the following, but do them anyway:

3. Decide on immediate changes you can make to improve effectiveness:

    I can stop doing _____

    I can better understand why _____

    I can improve the way _____

Adapted from Ralston, *Hidden Dynamics*, 1995.

4 Getting Started

Anyone who has suggested a change or tried to initiate a new program in an institution knows some of the roadblocks that can quickly appear. Starting an SEL program brings concerns to the surface. Will paying attention to social or emotional concerns detract from the academic program? Is there time for it? Will teachers (and students) be interested?

In this chapter, we will look at some of the ways to build support for an SEL initiative that can help you deal with the potential roadblocks. Addressing concerns of all constituencies, and seeking their assistance, will help inspire support and confidence as you begin an SEL initiative. Figure 4.1, a worksheet for administrators, highlights some of the issues that are explored further in this chapter.

GETTING FACULTY INPUT

A school initiative in social and emotional education requires engaging the members of the faculty and administration in a discussion of students' needs in this area, consideration of how the school is meeting them, and an exploration of possible benefits to expanding the way(s) those needs are addressed. The most important element of a successful program is a high degree of commitment, by the professionals involved, to including social and emotional skill development as an integral part of a quality education.

Before introducing any new program, it is essential to engage faculty in consideration and discussion of the proposal. This is certainly true for social and emotional education. The good news, however, is that most teachers today readily see a clear need for explicit attention to this topic and recognize the potential benefits for students, school climate, and the faculty themselves.

Small-Group Discussions

There may be no more effective way to garner faculty interest and enthusiasm than by asking them first to consider student needs. Ideally, this is done in groups small enough that teachers actually can think and converse with one another—from the point of view of concerned adults and parents, not simply as professional colleagues. Why? When faculty members come together to

29

FIGURE 4.1. Administrator's Worksheet, SEL and Decision-Making:
Schoolwide Activities

In proposing and designing schoolwide activities to enhance SEL instruction within the classroom, limitations of time, personnel, and finances often necessitate the establishment of priorities.

Consider the following when preparing to propose a new initiative:

1. Is the need for this activity supported by the administration and faculty's (students' or parents') perceptions of student needs? Does the activity address any needs that appear in school or district improvement plans?

2. Who will determine whether the proposal moves forward: faculty, administration, parents, students, or a combination of these groups?

3. What school personnel will be involved in the investigation of the issues related to implementing the proposed activity? Will the committee include students and parents? Will this group be charged with proposing solutions to potential implementation problems (e.g., personnel, finances, scheduling difficulties, etc.)?

4. Proposals have a better chance of implementation if research supports their effectiveness. Who will gather and review relevant literature and ensure the thorough review of issues related to this activity and its potential value to the students and school?

5. Who will formulate a final decision and design a plan for activity implementation?

---

consider the possibility of any initiative, the first instinct is often to articulate the potential problems that could develop. Consideration of the topic from a different perspective allows the possibilities to arise before the specter of real or imagined difficulties in implementation.

Participants in each small group should consist of members of different departments. This is particularly important in schools with many long-time faculty members who can almost predict the opinions of the other members of their department before hearing them. The discussion coordinator should be the program organizer, preferably a school leader with knowledge of, and interest in, the topic.

The direction these small-group conversations will take depends on the participants, but should include the following:

- Consideration of what the group considers a "successful" school year for students at the school
- A brief, introductory overview defining social and emotional intelligence and learning
- The group's observations concerning students' strengths and weaknesses in skills such as self-motivation and empathy, listening and delaying gratification
- A discussion of ways in which the school and the curriculum already provide students with opportunities to develop their self-awareness and interpersonal skills. Where do we already integrate SEL within our academic program? In what ways do we emphasize the importance of this dimension of our students' education, with parents, faculty, and the students themselves?
- Exploration of group members' interest in addressing some of these issues through expanded schoolwide programs and through limited, occasional infusion into academic disciplines. How does addressing these issues help us meet the goals of our school mission statement and/or district?

More specifically, questions these groups can begin with include the following:

- From your own experience, what strikes you about the level of social and emotional literacy of the students with whom you deal? Where have you seen concrete examples of individual (or group) strengths that particularly impress you? Are there specific weaknesses in these areas that come to mind? (Perhaps some stand out more than others.) Do any individual examples help illustrate your point(s)?
- Whatever your responsibilities at the school—teacher, counselor, administrator, coach, staff member—what do you already do in your own work to foster social and emotional health and awareness in the school, community, and among the students in particular?

- What initiatives are you aware of in the school at large that help promote education in this area?
- Consider your primary responsibility at the school. Are there other ways you could explicitly infuse social and emotional education into what you do? What problems and challenges might arise if you made such efforts? What kinds of professional development do you imagine would be most helpful for you?
- Consider the range of schoolwide student activities offered at your school. Are there any other specific programs that might help foster student awareness and experience in areas related to personal and interpersonal education?

After receiving faculty input, and having held a number of small-group discussions, you will be in a good position to evaluate whether you can move forward. It is likely at this juncture that you will be able to identify a core group of professional staff who believe that learning should include an explicit social and emotional education component. This group can help in a variety of practical ways to lay the groundwork for eventual program implementation.

Establishing a Steering Committee

When a consensus is reached that the school community will provide social and emotional education through specific schoolwide programs and the occasional infusion in academic courses, it is wise to consider the appointment of a program coordinator, who will chair the SEL steering committee. In addition to facilitating the organization of the program, the coordinator and steering committee provide orientation and training to new staff, while ensuring the maintenance and expansion of the program itself.

You should look for candidates among the staff who have the interest, organizational skills, and (professional) experience to help guide the development of the program and to serve as resources for faculty. During the first year of the program, in particular, it might be advisable to explore whether potential candidates might be allowed a reduction in their ordinary responsibilities, in order to further ensure that the first year is successful. Given the growing interest in and development of programs in social and emotional education, coordinators need the opportunity to network with other professionals in the field, stay current with the professional literature, and attend one or two conferences a year that will provide information on research trends and practices.

OVERCOMING RESISTANCE

"We don't have the time."
"I'm not interested."

"Will it take away from academics?"
"I'm not comfortable dealing with emotional issues."
"It's hard to blend it into my discipline."
"We already do it."
"Guidance and health should take care of this."
"It's the parents' responsibility."
"Will it make a difference?"

When you begin investigating the possibility of establishing a program in SEL, it is very common to hear such reservations and objections from teachers, parents, and others.

These concerns, whatever their source, need to be addressed from the start, in an open and nondefensive manner. Perhaps the most important point to emphasize is the fact that SEL clearly enhances the ability of a young person to improve her academic performance. Most of us can remember times when as young people we were so preoccupied with some personal or interpersonal issue that it was impossible to concentrate on schoolwork. Such a concern may seem silly and trivial to us now as adults, but distractions like these can have an immediate and emotionally engulfing effect on a child or an adolescent.

Emotional intelligence is crucial to healthy emotional and intellectual growth (Mayer & Salovey, 1997). Developing such intelligence through SEL programs is now recognized as an integral part of effective educational efforts to enhance the academic and social success of young people (Elias et al., 1997). SEL initiatives have developed from academic research on child development, in which emotional experience is used to help children develop skills that will facilitate their meeting life's challenges (Adams & Hamm, 1994; Carnegie Council on Adolescent Development, 1989; Sylwester, 1995). Those concerned that the intent of SEL programs is to replace the role of the family in the social and emotional education of the child need to understand that home collaboration, whenever possible, enhances the likelihood of successful learning in this area, in common with all others.

The issue of social and emotional learning is not tangential to education; students bring these issues to school, and like it or not we must help the students deal with them. The skills needed for students to focus in class, prepare for a quiz, or plan a long-term assignment hinge on their capacity to control their emotions, delay gratification, and plan their time. All of these skills are developed as part of a social and emotional education program.

Integration of SEL lessons into a school's curriculum is now viewed as essential for all students to promote their healthy emotional and social development. Action research programs such as the Improving Social Awareness/Social Problem Solving project (Elias & Clabby, 1992) illustrate the importance of teaching academic, social, and emotional skills in the class-

room. Programs that include SEL instruction within the classroom potentially can help children not only handle social problems, but also achieve
academically (Elias, Gara, Schuyler, Brandon-Muller, & Sayette, 1991).

By explicitly including instruction in emotional learning within academic
instruction, we increase students' capacity to grasp the connection between
what they are learning in the classroom and life itself. With the increasing com-
plexity of the world in which we live, this approach has the added advantage
of naturally promoting attention to multiple intelligences and multidisciplinary
teaching. Schools that have established programs report that once students
learn to control their impulses, they get along better, and teachers report
spending less time disciplining students and more time teaching them.

In the end, our goal in providing social and emotional education is to
provide students with exposure to, and practice with, skills that can enhance
their academic performance—and improve their chances for success in life.
Students who attend our schools should experience the fact that we are as
serious about promoting their emotional health and social skills as we are
about developing, for example, their mathematical ability.

Finally, the following guidelines will go a long way toward helping you
overcome much of the resistance you may encounter when initially proposing
and implementing an SEL program:

- Emphasize with all constituencies that promoting prosocial attitudes in
  students positively influences their academic progress and enhances the
  overall learning climate in the school
- Highlight and recognize all that is already being done in the school and
  by individual teachers to promote social and emotional learning
- Point out that SEL programs promote student participation
- Assure faculty and staff that the first year of the program will be a pilot
  year, and that their recommendations for improvement will be actively
  sought at the end of that time
- Start the design of this initiative even if you do not have 100% support
  and approval from every single member of the faculty and staff. You will
  rarely elicit the enthusiasm of everyone for *any* project, and you do not
  need it to develop a worthwhile SEL program.
- Seek faculty suggestions regarding the nature and scope of professional
  development needed in this area
- Publicize success and creativity in SEL instruction and program development whenever the opportunities present themselves
- Consider creative ways to promote SEL initiatives and reach out to others
  beyond the school, whenever possible, to include the participation and
  support of the larger community
- Raise topics for discussion with faculty from time to time that might serve
  to enhance the way the adults in the building relate to and support each

other, thereby acknowledging that the entire school is an "ongoing learning community" in the social and emotional domains

- Use annual evaluations to make adjustments to SEL programs and discuss program progress with constituencies inside and outside the school

GETTING STUDENT INPUT

Although they are often overlooked when educators develop program plans within a school, students themselves also can be a valuable and encouraging resource in the development of schoolwide social and emotional initiatives. Where possible and practical, invite students to participate in discussions regarding *their own* perception of student needs. To encourage their participation, rather than asking students to articulate their own concerns regarding social and emotional issues, ask them to explain what needs or issues they see among their peers—inside or outside school. Some students initially will be reluctant to participate in such a conversation, for a variety of reasons. Through the discussion of examples, consideration of new program possibilities, and demonstration of your interest in connecting academic education to life itself, students certainly can provide practical ideas and suggestions for program implementation. In the course of these discussions, be sure to recognize existing programs that already promote social and emotional learning within the school.

In the end, students can become not only valuable resources, but also some of the most enthusiastic supporters of specific school initiatives designed to foster their own social and emotional learning. Note the enthusiasm with which many students sign up to be leaders in programs designed to serve others, either within or outside the school. Such opportunities serve their own need to reach out to others, their need to be needed. Other students are delighted to promote school initiatives and programs by use of their artistic abilities. The more we tap into such energy, the more students we interest in our initiatives.

ATTRACTING SCHOOL LEADERSHIP

The school principal, as educational leader within the school, is the educator whose active support and involvement are most important. You also should consider other administrators and support personnel who are likely to have particular interest in the program and therefore might be likely to contribute to its organization and smooth running.

The way an administrator interacts with students, parents, faculty, and staff sets the tone for the way others in the building are expected to communicate. If the principal routinely treats others with disrespect and a lack of courtesy, even a well-organized program in social and emotional education has little hope of real success. We all recognize the hard work it requires for principals and teachers to meet the many requirements of their jobs, while also serving as reflective practitioners who can sustain real dialogue with one another—even when differences arise. When principals make daily efforts to communicate forthrightly and respectfully, to collaborate and support the work of faculty and staff, they go a long way in providing the essential leadership a schoolwide SEL program requires.

Informal leaders in the school community, both inside and outside the school itself, also can be important players in promoting program goals. Which parents tend to have an active interest in the school and its educational initiatives? What other district administrators, school faculty, and staff might have an interest in a budding SEL program? Touch base with these individuals, keep them informed in a general way, and seek their advice. Most adults readily see the value and practicality of fostering social and emotional intelligence, particularly when they understand that it enhances, not replaces or detracts from, all that is offered.

Administrative financial support will be necessary to cover the expense of professional development and the program coordinator's stipend. Who makes the financial decisions? Can the support of those individuals be enlisted as well? Are there outside community agencies and/or grants that might support this kind of educational initiative? Is there anyone connected with the school who has contacts with these organizations or has the ability to write a proposal for such a grant?

Perhaps the most valuable type of "supervision" that an administrator can provide is encouraging the professional self-reflection and self-evaluation of all involved in SEL instruction. Teachers should be encouraged to monitor the apparent effectiveness of the lessons they design and to share those reflections with colleagues working on the same project. During the first year of the program in particular, those lesson plans should be recorded on a computer; as time goes on, those deemed most effective by the teachers themselves should be compiled as an ever-expanding resource for all faculty, in particular those new to the staff.

Outside "supervisors"—ideally, members of the steering committee for the project—can help provide special assistance to individual teachers and can ensure that lessons are being carried out and implemented as intended. During the first year of the program's operation, teachers should be encouraged to have confidence in their abilities and to take instructional "risks." Time can be set aside during the second year to evaluate and make adjustments to work completed the previous year. The fundamental question is: How can we adjust or improve our lessons, in a practical way, to achieve our goals more effectively?

ATTRACTING DISTRICT LEADERSHIP

A schoolwide program in social and emotional learning will require district resources in the same way it will require the active support and involvement of administrative staff within the school itself. It is essential from the start to educate key personnel about the goals and purposes of the program.

Misconceptions can arise easily around the concept of social and emotional education, so it is particularly important that district administrators understand the purpose of such an initiative, if it is to become infused into the curriculum and promoted in various activities. Eventually, resource professionals from the district, including curriculum coordinators, can help establish clear objectives and assist with the development of ideas for various academic disciplines. Their active support and assistance goes a long way toward encouraging teachers to integrate emotional learning into their content curriculum.

School board members also provide a key liaison to the community and can aid in explaining and promoting this dimension of education within the school. For this reason, reports from the coordinator and committee implementing the program should be presented or written regularly, especially during the initial planning stages. Establishing a quarterly school newsletter that highlights program initiatives can be a worthwhile long-term goal for publicizing efforts and garnering support.

As the chief administrator for the school district, the superintendent plays a vital role in supporting social and emotional education within the school. The superintendent can help ensure program success by promoting the importance of social and emotional education as an essential component of all children's academic education, through the following avenues:

- Communicating support to the school administrators, faculty, and steering committee
- Publicizing this dimension of education within the community
- Pointing out how social and emotional education supports district goals
- Ensuring that the program receives administrative support and appropriate publicity

In effective school districts, schools often can function with a great deal of autonomy within the frameworks established by the district as a whole (Lambert, 1998). Certain schools within a district may elect to implement an SEL program; others may not. For schools that initiate a program autonomously, support of the district administration, through positive interest and communication with school personnel and the community, helps validate the importance of SEL as an integral part of the district vision for student learning.

In the end, any school program has a better chance of success if its goals clearly align with the educational priorities of the district and if it taps into the professional expertise available to support new school programs.

INVOLVING PARENTS

From the start, parents need to know what skills are included under the umbrella of "social and emotional education" and how students will be exposed to those skills within the school and curriculum. If parents understand the rationale for the program and how their children will benefit, they are likely to voice strong approval for the school's decision to give explicit attention to this dimension of education.

If possible, parent discussion groups—or a large-group assembly—can introduce parents to the concept of SEL. Parents see the need for it, but most will need education regarding the purpose of such education and how it will be offered within the school. District and school newsletters and local newspaper articles also can stir community interest—and pride—in such an initiative. Wherever possible, parents should be invited into the school to help with the initial planning, implementation, and evaluation of school programs in this domain; most of these parents will then become the strongest advocates for providing this type of education.

The school mission statement should be utilized with parents also, in explaining the purpose of program goals. Is there wording that provides explicit support for developing social and emotional learning? Course description booklets can note the specific skills that could be enhanced by the inclusion of a social and emotional component.

Some parents have the personal and professional background to assist with instruction; others have knowledge within the local community to serve as valuable resources in designing and developing SEL programs. When asked how they would like to assist, parents can express their natural interests, whether as mentors, fund raisers, or event coordinators.

Everyone connected with the school shares the same common interest in the education of young people. With an initiative as potentially helpful as a social and emotional learning program, the involvement of as many people as possible should be sought in the planning and program implementation process. It is also necessary to evaluate the attitudes and resources of the key decision makers inside and outside the school as you are proceeding with plans.

ANTICIPATING PROGRAM COSTS

A change as significant as implementing an SEL program requires a leader and organizer who can shield a new idea from the inevitable organizational torpedoes. This individual need not be the principal, but should be someone with the principal's support, the authority and skills to make things happen, and access to funds to support the program.

During the first organizational year and the initial implementation year, the most substantial cost is the salary or stipend that this individual receives. He will likely require a reduction in duties, such as teaching one less class or assuming one less administrative responsibility. This will allow time for teacher consultation and observation, follow-up discussions, schoolwide program organization, planning of professional development opportunities, and evaluation.

Professional development for faculty is the other major expense involved in initiating an SEL program. Each school and district operates differently, but a calculation of finances must include the cost of substitutes for teachers absent from school to attend workshops and the cost of those inservice experiences and of any consultants hired to visit the school.

The only other expense is that involved in stipends for those who organize or moderate a particular schoolwide activity, such as Big Brother/Big Sister. Providing the financial support for inservice opportunities and for moderators of schoolwide program signals the support of the central office and school administration for the SEL initiative.

As should be obvious, the costs of initiating an SEL program are minimal when we consider the potential benefits. The key is to have program leader(s) who are committed to developing students' social and emotional capacities and who have the interpersonal skills needed to build support for a new project.

UTILIZING RESOURCES

The Appendix contains a brief listing of resources that will be helpful as you approach the design of a social and emotional skills-building program. Speaking with individuals and groups working in this area can be the most valuable experience of all. The Collaborative for the Advancement of Social and Emotional Learning (CASEL) can provide information regarding relevant personnel, programs, and materials.

5 Schoolwide Activities: Initiatives That Work

Once there is agreement that developing students' social and emotional skills is an important undertaking, the school community must consider every avenue for addressing and reinforcing the skills it hopes to promote. The goals of such a program should be reflected in a total strategy that includes explicit incorporation of SEL in classroom lessons, deliberate working toward creating a respectful, caring environment within the school, and the implementation of appropriate schoolwide activities. In this chapter, we will look at a few such activities that have met with success.

Williamsburg Middle School in Arlington, Virginia, begins its schoolwide SEL program with community service in sixth grade, where students work with preschool children and senior citizens. In seventh grade, students work on environmental issues and with recycling organizations. By the time they have finished eighth grade, they are working on sensitive problems such as homelessness.

Why emphasize, in an SEL middle or high school, opportunities for student involvement and service? Peggy Brennan, a counselor at Yorktown High School, explains: "It is so clear that if students experience success in their connections with others—and we provide so many concrete avenues for this to take place—it will improve (for good reason) their self-esteem and thus their potential for achievement. When we think of large groups of students together in middle and high school, how many of us think of all they could be doing to get themselves in trouble? We are trying to create an accepting atmosphere and challenging opportunities, where students have a chance to experience the rewards inherent in doing the right thing. Our schoolwide initiatives hopefully provide a place for all types of students to feel good about themselves, what they are learning, and what they are doing."

SELECTED ACTIVITIES

A well-coordinated schoolwide program can increase students' self-awareness and provide them with opportunities to be needed within the school community. Especially as students grow older, the need to be needed grows in importance. That need can be met while simultaneously helping others within the school community.

A schoolwide activity should be selected because it meets the specific needs of a particular student body. How long should any single activity last? As long as it continues to meet the needs of students participating in it. Some suggested activities that have worked are described in the following sections. Each activity provides an educational opportunity, along with room for reflection and creativity. In the end, the number of activities a school can offer is largely a factor of the number of faculty available to serve as coordinators and moderators.

Setting Goals of Community Behavior

At schools like Yorktown and Williamsburg, student representatives, faculty, and administrators can meet over time to create what might be labeled a student-designed version of the school mission statement. While adults join the students in this undertaking, it is the students themselves who bear responsibility for creating the "code" they would like to promote within the school to guide behavior. Often, it is a variation on "respect for self, others and property"; the key point, however, is that students design and "own" it.

During the first week of school, student leaders who worked on the Goals for Community Behavior can explain them to peers. Determining how best to promote the goals among students becomes an important job. One school has students distribute wallet-size cards to every student in the building; another has an art contest with awards for the art that most creatively depicts the goals. This can then be used throughout the building, and on classroom doors, as yet another reminder of the student-created goals. With these symbols available, teachers also can refer to the goals as "teachable moments" arise.

Connecting School with Life

This connection can take many forms. From time to time, a faculty coordinator can work with students (and faculty) who have prepared in advance a brief 3- to 4-minute reflection that is presented over the school's public address or television system. That message, characterized by thoughtful preparation and designed to promote healthy, responsible living, should be presented at a time when all students *and* faculty are encouraged, even required, to cease activity and listen. This alone underscores the importance of taking a moment on occasion to calm down, pause, and listen to others. Such a pause in the week illustrates to students that we believe they, too, have something important to say; it reminds them, in ways as varied as the messages they hear, that we are educating them not simply for school, but for life. These reflections can cover a wide range of themes, but the guiding principle is that they challenge the members of the school community to think about how they are living their lives and to consider what decisions they are making or avoiding.

What can these reflections focus on? They can be as varied as the individuals who present them. One person speaks about friendship, another about something that happened to him or her that required hope or courage. Inevitably, some messages and stories are more compelling than others; unless one has experienced such a program, however, it is hard to appreciate what effective teachers the students themselves can be to one another. At times, the reflections bring life outside the school into the classroom, as it did on one occasion when a high school junior offered a rather sad and jarring life experience.

> The night before New Year's in Edgewood, the town where I was born and raised, David P. was stabbed. David and I grew up together, played on the same Little League team, and hung out until recently. But just as sad and shocking to me was that Greg, or Pizza—we called him Pizza because he worked at a pizza parlor—who lives across the street from me, was arrested for the murder. Now, David is dead and Pizza probably wishes that he was, too. They were friends. (Pasi, 1997)

After explaining the incident, this student then spoke for 2 minutes about the feelings and reactions this tragedy prompted within himself, including sadness for his friends and gratitude for his own life and situation. He wondered aloud why his friends didn't stop and think before reacting violently to each other. Not every reflection is so powerful, but each provides an opportunity for students and faculty to connect a lesson with life itself. These reflections also provide a means for students themselves to contribute, in a practical way, to the SEL program.

Organizing Big Brother/Big Sister Programs

It is so important to connect young people to their peers (and other adults) in relationships characterized by respectful, sustained caring. They need to feel others care for them, of course, but they also need opportunities to care for others. Many larger schools also face the challenge of personalizing students' daily experience in the building. One way of providing an opportunity for that personalization—for both older and younger students—is by organizing some type of Big Brother/Big Sister program. Such a program allows students the opportunity to reach out to others and to understand how others feel, while learning to recognize and respect differences.

This kind of activity needs one or two coordinators who will enlist student volunteers. Most students like any opportunity for a leadership experience, a feeling that they are needed; most schools report a surprisingly high number of student volunteers for opportunities where the older can help the younger. Some training in fundamental social skills is advisable. Students need to be taught how to actively take an interest in another, especially a peer who is shy or reticent. A faculty coordinator can design a brief, practical workshop that will help young people learn to forget themselves for a moment and reach out to another. In this way, they also learn new skills, thereby immediately benefiting from the program.

Once older students have been paired with younger ones, a variety of planned exercises can be arranged for brief, scheduled meetings. Students also can be encouraged to keep in contact with their younger peers informally, on birthdays and the like. Invariably, students new to a school state that this type of program is the best part of their orientation.

Organizing an Adult Advisor Program

This kind of program is meant to ensure that as few students as possible slip through the school year "anonymously." The number of students that can be included in such a program depends on the size of the school and the number of adult volunteers. Volunteers can be drawn from faculty, administrators, and any other professional staff in the building.

As part of this particular initiative, all students in a specific grade are informed of the existence of the program and their inclusion in it. Students who are active in the school, as part of an activity or sport, for example, are assigned their coach or club moderator as their "advisor" for the year. (This initiative is not designed for these students, who already have regular contact with at least one adult on the staff.)

It is designed, however, for students who do not participate in school life, who seem to have no connection with the school outside their attendance in class. (If this describes too large a segment of the school population, another means can be used to determine students ostensibly "on the fringe" of the school community.)

One coordinator of the program invites adult volunteers—administrators, coaches, and teachers—to agree to contact no more than three or four students at least once each academic quarter. These brief appointments are scheduled at the teacher's and student's mutually agreed-upon convenience, such as during homeroom or lunch, or before or after school.

While these faculty "advisors" are not meant to serve as counselors, they are meant to demonstrate concretely to students the active interest of a specific adult on the staff. As with the Big Brother/Big Sister program, counselors and administrators have a master list of these faculty/advisee pairings.

Should something of particular note or concern occur in the life of a student (e.g., a death in the family), the faculty advisor would be informed.

Presenting Theme-Based Assemblies

School assembly programs often focus on a particular social problem: substance abuse, teen pregnancy, drinking and driving, and so forth. Over time, these can come across to students as presentations on the "problem of the month." Another approach involves designing assemblies that address and reinforce skills students need to handle the variety of challenges they will confront with their peers. Such theme-based assemblies may focus not on a particular problem, but on the importance of skills like self-discipline, self-management, or communication when confronted with a wide range of decisions and situations. Interactive assemblies can include speakers who have used one or more SEL skills to surmount challenges or who have achieved some noteworthy accomplishment. The focus then is on the skills needed for successful decision-making in a wide variety of situations, rather than highlighting a series of distinct social problems. This requires the organization of the assembly program to help ensure that it is as integrated, comprehensive, and coordinated as possible.

Identifying Service Opportunities

Service learning acknowledges that young people have a role as resources for community problem-solving. It provides an opportunity to make the entire community a learning environment and offers the same type of leadership experience as an in-school program like Big Brother/Big Sister. There can be many activities under the umbrella of service learning, with either one coordinator for all or individual coordinators for each experience. However the activities are organized, students should be given the opportunity to practice caring and connecting with the world around them as contributors.

In addition to the experience provided by contributing one's time and talent in a practical setting, students should be provided ongoing opportunities to reflect upon what happened during their experience and as a result of it. These conversations with peers, guided by the adult coordinator, can provide rich insights and a real opportunity for young people to learn from one another and their experiences.

Creating Transition Groups

These groups, led by a counselor or faculty member, provide a structured opportunity during the first month of school for students new to the building, who may benefit from extra support. These students can be identified from school records or contact with counselors and/or administrators from feeder schools. It is not necessary to set an agenda ahead of time; often, these students will come in with an agenda of their own. The key is for the leader to express his or her interest in ensuring that every group member experiences success in his or her new educational setting and recognizes the importance of addressing problems that (inevitably) arise as soon as they occur.

Keeping Athletics in the Loop

In schools with an extensive athletic program, it is essential that the coaching staff operate with the same fundamental philosophy that the faculty and administration do during the school day. Students do not benefit when they receive contradictory messages from administrators, teachers, and coaches about what is or is not acceptable behavior between adults and students and among students themselves.

Prior to each season, administrators trying to promote social and emotional learning should arrange to meet with coaches to discuss the school's philosophy regarding sportsmanship, acceptable behavior, coach–student relationships, and ethical behavior.

The school's director of student activities can take a further, practical leadership role by designing a special contract for student athletes and their parents/guardians that outlines player guidelines and school behavioral expectations of all student athletes. Finally, a student athlete "goals sheet" might require every athlete to commit him- or herself to personal and team goals in several areas, both during and after the season.

Establishing Peer Mediation or Conflict Resolution Programs

Programs that engage students in helping mediate or resolve conflicts among their peers have been shown to be particularly effective in decreasing class violence, fostering a more positive and caring environment, and improving student communication skills. Like the Big Brother/Big Sister program, these initiatives help those involved in the mediation as much as they do those students who are being served. Counselors, trained teachers, or administrators can provide the preliminary training and monitoring these programs require. Many schools have such student-led services, and a large number of universities will provide literature and/or personnel to help local schools establish peer mediation or conflict resolution programs. In some counties, the Department of Human Services will provide staff to train students as peer educators for HIV/AIDS or violence prevention.

Planning Special Events

On occasion, a specially designed event or "day" can highlight a skill or concept you might like to, but ordinarily cannot, address with all students, or a
particular grade. Special "Wellness Days" can provide opportunities to focus
on a wide range of topics that fall under the domain of social and emotional
health. Programs at the start of the year for high school seniors, for example,
can provide a focus and direction for the important decision-making that will
take place during the upcoming year. This type of event can be designed to
meet the needs of students at all grade levels.

For example, at some schools the faculty makes a commitment to recognize students who demonstrate superior social and emotional intelligence—in the same way that they recognize students who demonstrate superior academic intelligence or athletic skill. "Principal's Breakfasts," in most
schools, honor students with the highest grades for a quarter. At Yorktown
High School, those students with academic grades of A in every subject are
recognized the first quarter, and those with the most improved academic
grades are honored the second. However, it is the third Principal's Breakfast
of the year that seems to attract most attention among students, faculty, and
parents. At this event, every faculty member selects one student who has
"contributed to the school climate and atmosphere in the way he or she deals
with others." In one case, a teacher selected a student who "routinely defuses
hostile interchanges with his gifted sense of humor." Another teacher selected a student who "quietly and routinely always assists those with special
needs in our class."

THE ROLE OF ADMINISTRATORS: DISCIPLINARIANS

In many schools, the burden of disciplinary responsibilities falls on the shoul-
ders of one or more administrators. Individuals in these positions who model
emotional intelligence provide the most important teaching strategy of all.
The key way in which an administrator teaches is by his demeanor—the way
he handles the conflicts that inevitably arise. In word and action, the administrator is in the most visible position to promote a school environment in
which everyone is expected to enhance, rather than diminish, the dignity of
others.

With regard to school discipline, a school that decides to promote social and emotional learning need not necessarily adjust existing penalties for
violations of school rules. But there are ways to use the discipline program to
reinforce students' social and emotional skills. For example, we use "student
decision sheets" (see Figure 5.1) as part of the in-school suspension program
at Yorktown. Students who have been involved in impulsive or aggressive

FIGURE 5.1. Student Decision Sheet

1. a. What problem occurred?

    OR (in the case of a pending incident that has not yet taken place)
    b. What is bothering you?

2. a. What did you do?

    OR
    b. What are you thinking of doing?

3. a. What happened after you acted?

    OR
    b. What do you think will happen after you act?

4. a. What did you do that worked well?

    OR
    b. What do you think is good about your plan of action?

5. a. What about your actions did not work out well?

    OR
    b. What might be a problem with your plan of action?

6. a. What could you have done differently that would have been better?

    OR
    b. What else could you do to handle the problem more effectively?

7. How do your actions — or your planned actions — fit in with the school's Goals for
    Community Behavior?

behavior are required to meet with an administrator or counselor to reflect on and discuss what led up to the disciplinary action and exactly what choices they made before and during the incident.

An administrator's worksheet (Figure 5.2) also serves as a record and a simple reminder to incorporate some SEL component when disciplining students for referrals caused by poor decision-making (that does not merit their suspension from school). This approach to discipline uses the problems and conflicts that arise to engage students in considering alternative responses that are reflective, nonviolent, and creative.

Students must individually record their responses to several questions, requiring of them an examination of what led up to the incident, how they behaved, and what alternatives they could have chosen. By requiring students to complete these sheets and then discuss their behavior, we help them learn to be aware of their feelings, to think about what those feelings mean, and to pause before choosing a course of action. An exploration of possible alternative solutions that could have been chosen concludes the session.

Some administrators in charge of discipline will not have time to consult with students in this way. It is time well spent, however, and will likely reduce the number of student referrals in the future. When the disciplinarian cannot allot time for this follow-up activity, a counselor or alternative administrator should serve as substitute.

THE ROLE OF COUNSELORS: FLEXIBLE RESOURCES

Counselors are in a unique position to serve as a valuable resource to teachers, administrators, and students alike in the important goal of fostering social and emotional competence within the school community. By virtue of their educational background and professional role, they can provide the implicit and explicit leadership a successful program requires.

Like the teacher in the classroom, a counselor's imagination is all that limits her from creatively contributing as a resource. Some activities counselors engage in include:

- Following up disciplinary referrals and incidents with a "student reflection" form that requires students to consider what took place before a particular incident, how they responded, and how they could react more constructively in the future. (In addition to assisting the student, such an activity fosters healthy counselor–administrator collaboration.)
- Informing faculty of their availability to visit classes to teach some component of social/emotional learning. This provides an opportunity for a counselor to deal with an entire group of students and demonstrates to

FIGURE 5.2. Administrator's Worksheet, Including SEL in Disciplinary Actions

Date: _____

Student's Name: _____

Grade: _____

Teacher/Staff Member Reporting Student: _____

Administrator's Name/Title: _____

Nature of Offense:

Additional Teacher/Staff Comment(s):

Student's Account:

Disciplinary Action:

SEL Activity—Description:

Date of SEL Activity Completion: _____

Including SEL in Disciplinary Action:

Student Statement:

I had a chance to tell my side of the story:_____

                                                                    (signature)

The purpose of the SEL activity, as I understand it, is as follows:

How would I behave more constructively in the future, given a similar situation?

faculty the counselor's willingness and ability to contribute in the class-room setting

- Working as consultants to administrators regarding ways to enhance the educational component of school disciplinary policies
- Empathizing and assisting parents who are frustrated with their child's repeated pattern of poor decision-making
- Communicating availability and assisting teachers in their planning of lessons that focus on social and emotional competence
- Consulting with teachers regarding ways to maximize student motivation to learn, such as promoting cooperative learning
- Serving as a resource to administrators and faculty in the distribution of articles and/or videos on topics related to social and emotional education
- Offering limited sessions of group activities that provide opportunities for listening and learning to respect one's own and others' points of view
- Organizing special workshops and programs that foster social and emotional competence: leadership workshops, peer mediation, conflict resolution groups, and so on.
- Encouraging the use of journals by student counselees; helping students who feel they "can't," learn that they "can" (feel more capable)
- By word, action, and example, helping to promote a decent, caring, and respectful school climate—a responsibility of all.

6 SEL Across the Curriculum

In the past, the interpersonal skills and prosocial attitudes we associate with SEL were taught more often in the home. As society has changed, the school experience has had to evolve, as well. Within the classroom today, a truly first-rate education continues to include student mastery of the academic curriculum. It also includes an environment, instruction, and experiences aimed at helping young people become more personally and interpersonally competent.

When we integrate SEL lessons into the curriculum, we teach academic content while not ignoring the social and emotional dimensions of life and intelligence. Resistance to the idea of adding "something else" to the curriculum need not be a permanent obstacle to incorporating emotional education into academic lessons. Competent, experienced teachers quite naturally pose thoughtful questions, suggest connections, and deal with emotional components in many classes throughout the year. Taking a science or language or social studies unit and underscoring a lesson in emotional competence can enrich and enliven an academic lesson. In this chapter, we will consider some issues and examples related to classroom applications of SEL.

The five fundamental dimensions of emotional intelligence include the following:

1. Self-awareness—understanding one's own strengths and limits
2. Self-management—handling one's emotions well
3. Motivation—moving toward one's goals with hopefulness
4. Empathy—capacity to take another's perspective; caring
5. Social skills—ability to communicate, listen, and interact effectively

The choice of skills an SEL program will target should meet the needs of the students at a particular school and the situations and dilemmas that these students will likely face. This can vary from school to school, which is another reason the individual design of each program is important. With so many potential SEL skills to emphasize, the local school community (with the guidance of the steering committee) ultimately must decide which set of skills will be promoted over another. Many SEL programs emphasize the importance of skills needed for intelligent decision-making and problem-solving, or qualities like empathy and tolerance. Within the classroom, teachers can use the problems that inevitably arise among students to help them learn how to interact with others more effectively. The use of role-playing and the practice that comes from working cooperatively in groups promote skills that students can generalize to other situations. When students are provided classroom opportunities to solve problems, and learn how to disagree with each other constructively, they also learn skills they can generalize to situations outside school.

The decision to bring SEL into the classroom—at any level—requires that faculty have the opportunity and time to design lessons that can be incorporated into their academic discipline(s). Model programs and lessons that are publicly available, such as *The PATHS Curriculum* (Kusché & Greenberg, 1997) and *Second Step: A Violence Prevention Curriculum* (Committee for Children, 1994), can serve as valuable resources. Even these, however, may not meet the specific needs of a teacher interested in integrating SEL into a particular academic lesson. Fortunately, most experienced teachers have often prepared the types of lessons necessary for the inclusion of SEL in their academic instruction. While these teachers are able to design SEL-inclusive lessons, they often need the confidence to appreciate the fact that they possess this ability. This confidence can encourage teachers to take instructional risks and use their imagination, two elements that are important to the success of any initiative in the classroom. Ultimately, student involvement will characterize many of these lessons, with their engagement in problem-solving or deducing understandings based on reflective experiences, literature, historical events, or discussions.

To begin, faculty should decide on a minimum number of lessons during the course of a year that they will devote to SEL. Students might receive, for example, four lessons in approximately seven different courses on the middle and high school level, providing them with a total of 28 explicit SEL classes. With the Goals of Community Behavior prominently displayed in every classroom, teachers naturally take advantage of other "teachable moments" during the course of the year to emphasize a skill or attitude related to SEL. Most teachers start the year by reviewing common expectations about classroom behavior; taken together, all these efforts increase the exposure students have to a broader definition of intelligence.

Although initially some teachers may express concern that even a couple of lessons could cut into precious class time, the consensus today is that the investment benefits academic learning. "Businesspeople tell us at every turn that one of the biggest problems they have with employees is their inability to get along with others because of their lack of skills, lack of self-awareness," says Diane Moore, business teacher at Yorktown. "It's so helpful to students that we acknowledge in the classroom that certain social skills are key to their future success in school and in life. It raises their awareness of how they conduct themselves in school, as well. In the end, I believe more learning occurs."

GROUPING SEL SKILLS THEMATICALLY

The set of skills that constitute a social and emotional curriculum have been defined in various ways, but usually include the following (Stone & Dillehunt, 1978):

- Self-awareness
- Decision-making
- Managing feelings
- Handling stress
- Empathy
- Communication
- Self-disclosure
- Insight (self/others)
- Self-acceptance
- Personal responsibility
- Assertiveness
- Group dynamics
- Conflict resolution

Similarly, the New Haven Social Competence curriculum focuses on three areas:

- Skills: self-management, problem-solving, and communication
- Attitudes and values: self, others, and tasks
- Content areas: self/health, relationships, and school/community

Others (Payton et al., 2000) organize a framework for SEL skills in the following manner:

- *Personal competence*—including self-awareness, self-management, and self-respect
- *Interpersonal competence*—including empathy and respect for others
- *Effective decision-making*—including goal-setting and problem-solving
- *Social interaction*—including communication and conflict management

These skills and attitudes, however categorized, all help students label their emotions and communicate them effectively to others. Along with academic learning, development of these skills helps students become truly knowledgeable and responsible persons.

Once you begin to narrow the focus of your school's program, the challenge becomes determining how best to infuse a particular skill or skills into instruction of the academic discipline during specific lessons. Many teachers already include components of this "universal" curriculum, even if they do not do so explicitly. For these teachers, explicitly stating the specific purpose of the lesson, in terms of social and emotional learning, is often a crucial piece that needs to be added.

When planning, keep in mind the overall goals of the SEL program and consider how your work in the classroom can contribute to achieving these goals. What specific themes and related skills do you want to target with the particular grade level you are teaching? An example drawn from the originally designed 4-year plan at La Salle Academy, Providence, Rhode Island (Figure 6.1), illustrates the potentially unifying effect of a common theme.

In that example, note that the theme of "decision-making" is the one common thread found in all 4 years. The faculty committee that decided on the final themes determined that making good decisions was the crucial social skill that students needed to work with throughout their 4 years of high school and would serve as the common thread for other skills selected for special attention.

Whatever the specific content of a class, or the strategy a teacher employs to communicate the material, numerous opportunities arise to teach students how to recognize their own feelings and those of others, how to listen and consider another's point of view, and how to appreciate the role

---

FIGURE 6.1. The Unifying Effect of a Common Theme

Grade 9—Theme: Decision-Making and Understanding Self.
Related skills: learning from mistakes, delaying gratification, developing positive self-concept, calming oneself, etc.

Grade 10—Theme: Decision-Making and Understanding Others.
Related skills: learning to listen, ways to relate to others, giving and accepting feedback, effects of stereotyping and prejudice, etc.

Grade 11—Theme: Decision-Making and Problem Solving.
Related skills: thinking before acting, steps in the problem-solving process, skills to enhance collaboration, evaluating future plans, etc.

Grade 12—Theme: Decision-Making, Service, and Leadership.
Related skills: appreciating diversity, developing empathy, implications of decision-making, etc.

---

of empathy in their own lives and in the lives of others. Opportunities abound in most all disciplines to teach academic content, while incorporating a message about self-acceptance, problem-solving/decision-making, or interpersonal relationships.

Teachers also might be encouraged to consider the possibility of adding a "home dimension" to lessons and activities. Part of an assignment could involve students' having to ask a parent, guardian, or sibling for an opinion or reaction to some aspect of the SEL lesson. Most experienced teachers have a natural ability to identify areas within their disciplines where they can draw a specific connection to a core SEL skill.

Department meetings can raise awareness of how teachers can focus conscious attention on the themes decided on for their particular year(s). Interdepartmental discussions also can generate ideas and possibilities for implementing social and emotional learning experiences into the classroom in an effort to reach both the heads and the hearts of all students. Administrators and others who observe a class can serve as thoughtful resources to help teachers reflect on their lessons (see Figure 6.2, Administrator's Worksheet).

RECOGNIZING OPPORTUNITIES FOR SEL INSTRUCTION

Students learn social and emotional skills—in the classroom and via special school programs—through three elements: example, experience, and reflection. These varied modes of learning develop skills in distinct yet complementary ways.

- *Example*: As a responsible adult and teacher, you are in an influential position to serve as a role model yourself each day, while also pointing to other role models who appear able to handle, in an intelligent and self-controlled manner, the conflicts that inevitably arise in life.
- *Experience*: Consider your curriculum. Where and how is it possible to present students with opportunities for problem-solving, decision-making, and analysis?
- *Reflection*: On occasion, provide time for students to slow down and experience the importance of personal reflection as a means to making wiser choices in school and life. If we don't provide the time, some never take it.

During the initial stages of planning a program, faculty members need to appreciate that their professional experience and understanding of children goes a long way toward helping them effectively infuse their instruction with a social/emotional component, directly or indirectly. Far too frequently, talented and experienced teachers do not give themselves credit for all they know and can do, trusting an outside expert more than their own teaching

**FIGURE 6.2. Administrator's Worksheet, SEL and Problem-Solving:
            Helping Teachers Engage Students**

One effective way of incorporating SEL into instruction, and increasing the engagement of students, is the use of problem-based learning in the classroom. This sheet can help you serve as a resource and guide to teachers engaged in this work.

1. What is the teacher-designed or student-designed problem? Is it engaging? Does it cover material related to the curriculum, while including an SEL dimension?

2. What is the SEL skill or dimension reinforced in this lesson?

3. How do students serve as investigators of their problem or decision? Does the teacher guide or coach students in this process?

4. Do students have the opportunity within the lesson to implement the following:

   • investigate needed information?

   • generate possible solutions?

   • suggest a problem resolution?

5. In what ways does the teacher serve as an effective coach or guide?

_____listens actively

_____questions thoughtfully

_____gives time for thoughtful responses

_____promotes student-to-student conversation

_____challenges data, assumptions, and biases

_____manages groupwork effectively

6. In what ways are the activity and its goals consistent with the school and district mission plan, strategic plan, and established curriculum?

7. Can the activity be implemented with existing school financial and personnel resources? If not, are there additional sources available for funding?

8. When will the activity be implemented?

9. When and by whom will the activity be evaluated?

strengths. In reality, many of these same teachers are the most perceptive individuals regarding the needs of their students. They understand from daily contact the most effective ways to integrate SEL lessons into their curriculum and instructional delivery.

As teachers grow in their experience of infusing social and emotional learning into their classes, they will increasingly appreciate the many opportunities there are for them to do so. In many disciplines, occasions arise where one or more of the following strategies can be employed using the media as a starting point:

- Using a film or video segment (related to the curriculum for a particular class) to examine reality (e.g., What approach did these characters take in solving that problem? Was it effective? What other alternatives could they have employed? How accurately does a particular interaction reflect the way you interact with each other, or the way others you observe react with each other?)
- Considering with students whether there are any implicit messages in what otherwise might appear a straightforward media presentation
- Incorporating music, print, or television commercials when considering a particular social skill or emotional reaction to a situation
- Considering personalities the media promotes as heroes or villains: What qualities are implicitly being promoted or disdained?
- Examining incidents of violence or kindness from the news as an impetus for considering alternative approaches to conflict resolution
- Using examples of responsible decision-making as they arise in the study of health, social studies, literature, science, and so on. In one business class, a successful entrepreneur's reasons for changing his fundamental approach to his employees triggered a discussion about the value of mutual respect among people regardless of their position in life.

Some disciplines lend themselves more naturally to an incorporation of lessons in social and emotional learning. Certain teachers have a greater facility for finding opportunities within the syllabus to highlight SEL lessons. It's not always easy. Providing opportunities for professional collaboration and appropriate inservice activities, however, can help those who have more difficulty and will encourage those who have been creative in their classroom approaches to share their successes.

SELECTED ACTIVITIES

Once themes and skills have been determined for a particular grade, class, or year—depending on the most practical way to organize the program in a school—activities and lessons should be selected that promote the specific agreed-upon goals. Teachers collaborating within the same department generally can accomplish this most effectively; it requires a block of time for initial brainstorming.

The coordinator and/or steering committee should be available to assist teachers in securing any special instructional resources (e.g., videos, materials) that would help them meet their goals.

Principles to Remember

Anyone who works in schools appreciates the high level of industry and seriousness of purpose that effective teachers bring to their work each day. To ensure that they do not overburden themselves with unreasonable expectations when integrating social and emotional education into their classes, it is important that teachers keep in mind a few general principles.

1. *A "cookbook" approach to teaching emotional intelligence does not work.*

Teachers themselves design the most effective lessons for infusing their discipline with instruction in social and emotional learning. Most experienced teachers readily appreciate the opportunities within their discipline to teach students the importance of learning self-control, showing respect, and acting responsibly. The creative component they bring to the lesson is more important than the "directions" that may be spelled out in a teacher's manual.

2. *The amount of time a teacher must spend outside the normal framework of her lessons should be minimal.*

The goal is not to change a science course into a course in emotional learning, but to use the content of a science class or some aspect of the scientific method to reinforce, on occasion, a specific principle of social or emotional learning. A few specific lessons, and other opportunities that naturally arise from time to time, can help students develop an awareness of their own emotions and the skills they need to deal effectively with others. A common error is to "overdo" one's efforts during the first 3 or 4 weeks of school. It is more effective in the long run to plan an occasional lesson and point to specific applications as they arise throughout the year.

3. *The content of some academic disciplines lends itself more naturally than others to the application of social and emotional education.*

A teacher of English can quite naturally infuse a lesson on the importance of delaying self-gratification into a writing lesson or discussion of a piece of literature. This is more difficult for a teacher of mathematics. However, teachers of any content area have occasions to emphasize, directly or indirectly, hallmarks of social and emotional intelligence, such as self-awareness, impulse control, zeal, self-motivation, empathy, persistence, and so forth. Teaching students to control themselves and calm down in the heat of a debate or discussion, when emotions are running high, can be an invaluable lesson they can apply to other (out of school) situations. It does require that the teacher take the time to focus on that skill when the opportunity presents itself.

4. *The effort will be worthwhile.*

Students who learn to develop an awareness of how they feel, how others feel, and how their behaviors affect others, become more able to calm down and think when confronted with challenging situations. Helping students develop this awareness and self-control forms a solid foundation for teaching them steps in making good decisions and solving problems.

5. *The skills must be modeled as well as taught.*

The extent to which faculty and staff regularly practice positive social and emotional skills, among themselves and with students, significantly influences how students themselves respond to SEL instruction and initiatives. It is difficult to promote self-control and respect for others among students if the administrators and faculty do not exercise those qualities themselves. Students tend to pick up on such contradictions!

6. *Recognize that a new program also must be considered an evolving one.*

Some things will work very well during the first year of program implementation, others less so. Helping students develop social and emotional competence takes time, trial, and error. At times, the task seems daunting. For this reason alone, everyone involved must recognize along the way the importance of sharing what works and what does not.

7. *Don't presume that students have mastered such important, basic skills.*

As a teacher and administrator, I have been surprised on many occasions to see older adolescents quite engaged in learning such skills as how to focus and listen, how to self-motivate, and how to empathize—all skills I would have presumed they already knew.

8. *Think about class dynamics as well as class content.*

Although the content of a particular class often lends itself to illustration or discussion of a social or emotional principle, on other occasions the nature of the instruction itself can be the pedagogical tool. Explicit comments from the instructor on roles and dynamics within group situations, or cooperative learning experiences, can prove helpful and educational to students. An appropriate mix of whole-class, individual, and group instruction provides varied opportunities for highlighting the importance of certain skills and behaviors, depending on the setting. A teacher can provide a valuable lesson, for example, by modeling effective listening and encouraging students to do the same. Teaching methodologies provide as many opportunities for applications of social and emotional learning as does content.

9. *Be explicit.*

When an occasion arises to reinforce some aspect of emotional learning, do not assume students will quickly or naturally pick up the implied message of the lesson, material, or classroom activity. If you are not explicit, the point you hope to make will likely be lost. For example, explicitly underscore how a historical figure succeeded because he had the discipline to delay gratification. Make what's implicit more explicit.

10. *Broaden the frame of reference to the whole school.*

When an appropriate "teachable moment" arises, do not hesitate to refer to student-written Goals of Community Behavior, if the school has adopted such goals as part of its overall initiative in social/emotional education (see Chapter 5).

Selecting a Methodology

Let's presume you plan to teach a class in which you will infuse your discipline with a lesson in developing the skill of listening or developing empathy.

Make a choice: Will you incorporate the skill into the lesson through your pedagogical strategy (e.g., a cooperative group exercise) or through the subject content (i.e., the academic discipline itself)? As you ordinarily would, vary your method of SEL instruction to include the following:

Group discussions and debates
Script writing and role-playing
Reflection and journal-writing
Use of manipulatives and artistic expression
Reactions to media and other presentations

Whatever your strategy, when you begin class, clearly state your goals: "We will learn about World War II today, but we also will be learning an important social skill that can serve you well outside this class." Reinforce this *explicitly* at the end of the class, highlighting the social skill you wanted to cover and exactly how you tried to do this. The key point is to be unambiguous about your goals for the lesson.

Each SEL lesson should seek to achieve a specific objective, while utilizing the academic content as a means to that end. This objective, articulated by the teacher at the start and end of the lesson, offers students a clear understanding of the concept or skill under consideration. In science class, the SEL objective within the lesson could be the importance of flexible thinking when solving a frustrating problem. At the end of the class, the science teacher might challenge students to apply that skill to life outside the classroom. When have they had to think flexibly at home, at work, or with friends? The content of the class itself, however, might have dealt with conducting a science experiment that is not easily solved. A similar approach can be taken in other disciplines when students are challenged with a difficult problem: The content remains math, science, foreign language, and so forth. The objective of the lesson shifts slightly, however, as an SEL principle is highlighted at the beginning and end of the class.

Whatever the academic discipline, one key strategy is to personalize discussion questions so students must consider how they can apply in their own lives the concepts they have learned. This dimension of personalization helps students move from an intellectual understanding of a skill or attitude (e.g., empathy) to a felt understanding of how such learning can assist them in dealing with the challenges of life in and outside school.

Many of the lessons teachers plan use some aspect of the curriculum to also encourage students to look at themselves, their attitudes, and their approach to life's challenges. It becomes essential, therefore, that an atmosphere of trust and mutual respect be promoted within the classroom from the first day. In many effective classrooms, teacher and students will have agreed on the ground rules for behavior when school starts. When students' behavior steps outside those guidelines, an effective teacher tends not to ignore what is inappropriate. A real challenge for teachers, especially in a classroom and school conscious of SEL, is the need themselves to be authentic, to recognize when they have been rude or offensive, or have acted without thinking. As we know, students learn best from example, and they will learn some powerful lessons from a teacher who is unafraid to acknowledge his or her own mistakes when they occur during the year.

CLASSROOM APPLICATIONS

Applications of social and emotional learning to different academic disciplines are as limitless as a teacher's imagination. As always, a stimulating and nurturing classroom environment, opportunities for experiential learning, and frequent feedback form the foundation of successful instruction. Perhaps some of what follows will provoke ideas related to the particular grade or academic discipline(s) with which you work.

Middle School Classes: Across Disciplines

Middle school teachers are often more accustomed than high school teachers to designing activities that require groupwork, discussion, and interaction. Students in early adolescence require a particularly high level of involvement with their peers, and middle school teachers (who often plan lessons as part of a team with their colleagues) understand that need. The following activities are not grouped by academic discipline, but can be modified to fit the needs of varied subject areas. All are intended to increase the level of students' self-awareness, self-acceptance, and understanding of emotions. Changes and adjustments may be required to ensure that activities are appropriate for particular classes and groups.

Most of these lessons contain a stimulus activity or problem-solving situation, followed by discussion or reflection. As with all SEL classes, it is wise to explain the lesson's objective at the start and end of the lesson. Do not presume that the point of the lesson will naturally be understood; it is important to require students to generalize what they have learned from the lesson and apply it to their lives outside school. In a typical 45- or 50-minute class, the stimulus or presenting problem often may take the first 15 or 20 minutes of class time, with the remainder available for discussion. The value of the discussion time is that it also allows students to practice the very skills they are considering: how to listen, problem-solve, and make good decisions; how to better understand themselves and others; how to think before acting.

- Use a story from the newspaper or local TV news in which a young person did something foolish, even dangerous, because someone else dared her to do it. Students frequently like to share their own stories or incidents that happened to their friends. Discussion eventually should focus on what makes students feel good about themselves and what makes them respect others.
- Have students identify the various dimensions that make up each individual: physical, intellectual, emotional, spiritual, social. How can they artistically represent the dimensions they feel are their greatest strengths? Brainstorm together the ways a person could develop any of those domains he would like to improve. Clarify that every person has strengths and weaknesses in each area.
- Consider a character in literature, history, or the news who did something she believed in, even though it resulted in criticism from others. Has the student ever been in such a situation? A friend? When is peer pressure (so prevalent at this age) a positive force? When is it a negative influence? What

are effective ways to deal with peer pressure? Do students respect those who resist the pressure of their peers?

- Have students create a "Day in My Life" log, starting with the time they get up in the morning and ending with the time they go to bed. Pair students up and have them consider and discuss where they have control in their lives and where they do not. Toward the end of the lesson, have them focus on the particular areas in their life where they *do* exercise personal power and the freedom to make decisions.

- Ask students to choose one person in their life whom they admire—a celebrity, family member, friend, or acquaintance. What are the qualities about that individual that they admire—a specific ability or personal quality? What is one ability or quality that they respect about themselves? Finally, what is the connection between our abilities, qualities, and self-worth? How do we learn to feel worthwhile about ourselves, even in the face of failures?

- Conduct an individual reflective exercise: Ask students to consider a recent incident that made them unhappy, such as failing a test, arguing with a friend, or missing out on a social event. How did they respond to the disappointment? Did they take their anger out on someone else? Withdraw? What are the ways we can handle disappointments when they inevitably arise? Which ways are effective? Ineffective?

- Pair students. Ask them to share the incident from the reflective exercise or choose another experience that prompted disappointment or anger. Student A must listen to the situation Student B describes and may not interrupt. When Student A is finished, Student B should advise her on how she can view the situation in perspective. Students then reverse roles. What are the differences in the way we support others and the way we internally support ourselves? How could we improve the tendency most of us have to be supportive of others when something goes wrong, but negative and critical in what we say to ourselves about our own actions in similar situations?

- Seat students in groups of four. Instruct each group to brainstorm the many emotions we can feel during the course of a week, from sad to happy to self-pitying. Have them make two columns: those feelings they believe we *can* control, and those they believe we *cannot*. After 15 or 20 minutes, have one representative from each group go to the board and record the group's list for the rest of the class to see. In comparing groups' lists and discussing them, help students see how we can control our thoughts—and feelings—in more situations than we often realize.

- Write on the board: "Anger is a choice." Divide students into groups of four to six participants and ask them to come to a decision on whether they agree with that statement. In their small-group discussions, they must use one example from their own lives (in which they became angry) to support their point of view. Conclude the discussions with the entire class, asking the students how self-talk can be used to control anger.

- Divide students into straight lines of approximately four students in each line. Explain that they are going to experience how one negative situation can create a series of negative emotions. The first student should think of an event that would disappoint or anger the next person in line (e.g., you did not make the team; you did not win the election). The second student must then turn to the third, express the negative emotion he is feeling, and another negative thought the student might now have about himself (e.g., angry—"I will never make any team I try out for"; hurt—"I bet no one likes me."). The next student in line must come up with another (negative) thought in the feeling or chain. Discuss how the first thought influences subsequent thoughts. Do the exercise again with a more positive or constructive reaction from the first student. Discuss with the class how our thoughts affect our feelings and how we can change our feelings by changing our thoughts about an event.

- Ask students to give an example from a recent TV show or movie in which one of the characters experiences something upsetting. How did the character handle the upsetting experience? If the character handled it poorly or well, what was she responding to that affected her emotional reaction (and behavior)? How can you apply this example to situations you will confront in the future?

- Divide students into small groups. Each group must make a list of school rules, family expectations, or community laws that they must follow. After the list has been compiled, they must imagine a scenario where one of those rules has been broken (e.g., underage drinking, cheating on a test, stealing from a store). What would be the likely consequence(s) for each violation? Discuss these as an entire class, having a student list some of the imagined consequences on the board. End the class with a discussion of the need to think before acting, and how students can apply the lesson regarding consequences to their own behavior and lives.

- As a variation on the foregoing lesson, have students consider the impact of their actions on others. Have small groups of students create scenarios in which something they do, or fail to do, has a negative consequence for a friend or family member. Conclude the class with a discussion of how our behavior affects ourselves and others, and the importance of thought before action.

- Divide the class into two groups. Each group must create events that would disappoint any of their peers (e.g., a fight with a friend, poor grades, family problem). After 15 or 20 minutes, a student from Group A states one of the disappointing or upsetting situations to the students in the other group. Students from the other group must identify negative thoughts, feelings, and behaviors the situation could prompt, and then positive ways to challenge the negative thoughts and feelings that otherwise could take over. Conclude the class with a discussion of the importance of challenging negative thoughts and working at replacing them with more positive, constructive ones.

- Ask the class to come up with a character from a popular TV show or recent movie who made a decision or tried to solve a problem while upset. What was the situation? How did the character respond? In the course of the discussion, raise students' awareness of the impact our emotions have on our decision-making and problem-solving abilities. Consider alternative courses of action for the characters they mention.
- Require students to list every means at their disposal, from parents to computer, to investigate the short-term goals they must reach on their way toward achieving a long-term goal. First, discuss the meaning of a goal and have them select one possible long-term goal they might have in life (e.g., becoming a professional athlete or president of a company; contributing to an emotionally healthy home; rearing healthy, confident children). Their assignment is to break that long-term goal down into short-term goals they first must reach along the way. As students eventually begin discussing personal long-term goals and steps they must take to reach them, emphasize the importance of self-discipline and short-term goals on the road toward achieving meaningful accomplishments.

High School Classes: Within Academic Disciplines

In the secondary classroom, we cannot abandon the goal of promoting student academic achievement along with attention to their *continuing* progress in intrapersonal and interpersonal growth. This requires the planning of engaging lessons connected to students' interests and experiences, and the establishment of caring, respectful communities in each classroom throughout the school.

As high school educators, we can play a crucial role in helping our students improve their social and emotional skills. We must be patient in our efforts, recognizing how long it takes to develop most of these skills. Our students, like ourselves, have developed into the persons they are over many years. It would be naive for us to think we could improve their self-management skills, as an example, with just one well-prepared lesson. Appreciating this fact, we approach our work with SEL skills understanding that we confront the same challenges we face when teaching other complex lessons. In an SEL school, one big advantage is knowing that other teachers are confronting the same challenge we face, perhaps from different angles.

The following strategies can be used across disciplines to help create a classroom environment and learning opportunities that will foster SEL.

Recognize Individuality.

At the start of the academic year or new semester, explain to students in general terms what they will be learning and how they will be assessed. Ask them to respond as a large group, or individually in writing, about how they learn best, what interests them most (if anything) about the subject they will study, and what unique abilities they have that might be used in class. In starting the course in this way, teachers demonstrate that they are respectful of the diverse backgrounds, interests, and needs of students; this also can enhance student motivation to achieve in a particular course and students' regard for the teacher who has shown interest in them as individuals. This type of beginning also provides an opportunity to address the kind of classroom community of learners the teacher wants to establish, characterized first and foremost by respect for individual differences.

Acknowledge Distraction.

Motivation to learn is influenced, in part, by an individual's emotional state. On occasion, at the start of the class, acknowledge that fact. Pair students and ask them to consider how they are feeling and what might be preventing them from focusing on the lesson. First, students must actually consider how they feel and what label(s) they would give to that feeling. They then choose how much they wish to share with their partner. This simple opportunity to take just a few minutes to talk about how they feel at the moment can help a student dispel the distraction for the remainder of the lesson. True, this exercise takes a little time. The consequence of never providing such an opportunity, however, may be teaching a lesson to a completely distracted student who lacks the motivation to learn.

Guide Group Participation.

When using cooperative learning and group problem-solving in class, provide the entire class with guidance and feedback about group interactions. Take the time to ask students to identify which qualities characterize an effective group participant and which qualities detract. Publicly praise students with particular abilities in this domain and, when possible, individually advise students whose skills are lacking. Help the students understand how they can function more effectively when working with others. Ask students how developing these small-group skills can help them outside the classroom as well.

Analyze Decision-Making.

A variation on the previous exercise requires students to reflect on how effectively the group thought out possible solutions and planned a course of action. Ask each individual how he approached analysis of the problem and implementation of a solution. On occasion, have students write their analyses of themselves and the group. Ask them to consider what they learned about themselves or others that could help them in situations outside school.

Assist with Disagreements.

Devise lessons that require students to think critically, come up with different solutions to a problem, or present different approaches to an issue. Help them learn that having different opinions is fine and that learning how to express them respectfully to those who differ is equally important. When students tackle a discussion or issue that prompts varied opinions and reactions, they are inevitably more engaged than when they simply listen. After a lesson involving the sharing of different opinions, ask for students' reflections on the skill of disagreeing without losing their emotions. Ask students which is more difficult: controlling emotions when listening to someone disagree with them or when disagreeing themselves? How are such insights important outside the classroom? Lessons like these help students learn to attend to their emotions while reasoning.

Promote Engagement.

"Read, reflect, write, and respond." Students, like adults, prefer to be engaged in what they are doing. A simple exercise that can have wide applications requires students to read a news story related to the discipline being studied. This works best if the news story is controversial. Have students consider a question related to the story: What could the principal character in the story have done differently? Do you consider the main character right or wrong? Why? Students can debate the story or report it to the class as an editorial from their unique point of view. After one debate or presentation, have students reverse perspectives. Once again, students must practice reflecting on a situation that provokes reaction and then practice being disagreed with and disagreeing with others.

Consider Alternatives.

Not every lesson need deal with students learning to control their emotions. A discussion prompted by a piece of literature or historical event can prompt students to consider when more aggressive behavior might be helpful, even necessary. Students recognize that in school the less aggressive, less impulsive students tend to meet with more teacher approval. Asking students to consider the value of more aggressive responses, when attacked, for example, adds a different perspective than ordinarily is stressed.

Provide Practice.

Most disciplines provide occasions for students to speak with a member of the school, community, or their own family to deepen their knowledge and gain the perspective of another person. We live in an era when many students isolate themselves by listening to Walkmans and working autonomously at a computer terminal. Having students interview another person on a topic related to the course does more than help them learn how to take an interest in the opinions and feelings of others. It also can provide an opportunity to develop communication skills, assertiveness, and empathy. When students discuss the interview experience, highlight more than the content discussed during the interview. How did students cope with the stress such an assignment can engender? What techniques did they use to elicit the thoughts and opinions of their interviewees? What suggestions would they have for someone else embarking on such an assignment?

Collaborate.

In many schools, teachers work autonomously; academic disciplines operate in isolation. There are few multidisciplinary courses and little collaboration across departments. What opportunities are there between classes and courses for students and teachers to interact and collaborate, perhaps in the investigation of a problem whose dimensions span more than one discipline? How can students in a technology class collaborate with students in a government class to analyze and solve a problem together? These interdisciplinary approaches illustrate a commitment to improvement and innovation, and provide valuable experiences for students to work together. Students also learn and benefit from the modeling of teachers working together to integrate content areas.

Encourage Reflection.

Journal-writing assignments can be structured around articles from newspapers and news magazines that raise issues requiring problem-solving or decision-making. The length of writing is not as important as the students' getting to the heart of the issue and summarizing the different perspectives of the individuals involved. Students must state the issue or present it as a question and then give their personal recommendation for resolution (e.g., should the individuals in the news story be allowed to protest in the way they did?). Students must be prepared to use their writing to support their point of view in class with those who differ.

Examples by Subject

The few examples within specific disciplines that follow are hardly exhaustive; faculty who teach these disciplines every day know more about applicable SEL content than anyone else. What follows is meant to be illustrative of the types of lessons and strategies teachers interested in integrating SEL might use.

Computer Courses.

One problem the technological age has presented is that many young people spend more time alone in front of a computer screen than socializing or working cooperatively with others. Conscious of this, some technology teachers require students to show at least one peer the results of any individual work. When students conduct computer research to learn about a career or investigate a news story, they must share their findings with another student working on a different project. Other possibilities might include variations on the following types of activities:

- In order to promote self-awareness, students can design projects (using specific programs like Hyperstudio) that require them to reflect on their strengths, interests, talents, and hobbies. They can then use that skill to teach younger students how to access information from the computer.
- Using the steps involved in effective problem-solving, students can work cooperatively to implement a newly learned program. Some class time can be used on occasion to have students examine how they handle the frustration that arises when learning a new program, and providing them with the opportunity to hear how their peers handle it.
- When students develop their own personal, electronic portfolio, they can monitor their progress in reaching academic, extracurricular, and personal goals. This helps them develop an increasing awareness of, and sense of responsibility for, their own growing "record."
- Students can practice computer skills such as word processing and at the same time be encouraged to reflect along the way. Provide them with questions and answers that promote personal and interpersonal intelligence, and that will change over time (e.g., Why are you in school? Whom do you admire? What is one quality you respect about yourself?).
- In collaboration with a fellow teacher and students from another discipline, students can research and articulate conflicting perspectives on a social studies, health, or science topic. Students in a communications class may define the dimensions of a problem such as the media's right to free speech and an individual's right to privacy, and a technology student can provide peer assistance in methods for research and techniques of presentation.
- You might consider the possibility of inviting interested members of the community, including senior citizens, to assist students with projects in the computer lab. Such opportunities tend to benefit both students and older volunteers at the same time.

Social Studies.

Social studies classes provide many natural opportunities to help students gain multiple perspectives on events that have led to national and global problems. What events led up to the crisis? What personality characteristics of leaders may have influenced the decisions that they made? Were there other alternative possibilities? What can students learn about themselves and their relations with others today from the historical events and personalities they review and the emotions those events sometimes can still provoke?

- Small-group work might include activities such as different subgroups investigating different facets of a historical problem, with all groups rejoining to arrive at new solutions. What do students learn about problem-solving and decision-making? What competing needs and attitudes may not have been apparent at first? Many historical events lend themselves naturally to problem-solving analyses.
- Have students consider what personal qualities demonstrated by leaders helped or hindered the leaders in reaching their goals.
- Divide students into small groups to examine a current or historical controversy. Half the group researches and presents one side of the issue; the other group researches and presents the opposing view. After debate, in the small group or large class, students reverse positions. These experiences help students to learn how to handle their emotions while disagreeing, to understand different perspectives, and to manage conflict.
- Have students play the role of mediator in a historical or current national dispute. What skills does the mediator need? When do they need similar skills in their own lives?

Physical Education.

Engaging in competition or learning a new physical education activity provides many opportunities for students to recognize their emotions directly and explicitly. Many lessons lend themselves to activities that require group cooperation, and the dynamics involved in competition and teamwork provide natural material for teacher-led discussions. What are the social and emotional challenges for any of us involved in the heat of competition? How do we handle the disappointment of defeat or failure? What steps can we take to remain calm in the midst of frustration, even when provoked? Including discussions of these social and emotional dimensions after an activity in physical education shows that they are an important part of the SEL program.

Some universities and recreation centers offer outdoor programs in leadership challenges. Such programs mix various experiences of obstacle challenges with lessons on leadership and achieving one's personal best.

These provide excellent opportunities for experiential social and emotional learning that are engaging and appealing to many young people.

Music and Art.

Classes in music or art provide many opportunities for reflection on, and reinforcement of, the emotional content inherent in artistic expression. Consideration of the affective dimension of music promotes increased self-awareness and provides an avenue for the creative and appropriate expression of emotion. What feelings did that piece evoke? Do you think it was the same as the composer or musician intended? Have students share their perceptions with one other person. This provides students with practice in perceiving and identifying emotions, while learning that others can perceive the same stimuli differently.

As students create musical compositions and produce musical shows, they develop their expressive communication skills. The key to effective SEL instruction in the arts is the teacher's interest in and willingness to guide students in reflecting on the affective dimensions of their own creative expressions and those of others.

Teaching students to critique their peers' art projects is a concrete way of providing students with experiences in giving and receiving praise and criticism. Having students develop sketchbooks or visual diaries helps increase their self-awareness, while using a multicultural approach to art appreciation fosters a respect for diversity. When expressing themselves artistically, students can communicate a message indirectly that they otherwise may not choose to articulate. The art teacher has a special role in helping students explore and express their feelings in both direct and indirect ways.

Mathematics.

Teaching mathematics provides opportunities for an examination of the strategies we use when solving problems, the ways each of us handles frustration in problem-solving, and the varied strategies we can use when confronted with a challenge. Requiring students to articulate *how* they solved a problem can foster self-awareness and insight. Phrasing word problems in ways that reinforce emotional learning is a practical way of bringing SEL into the math classroom. Many math students need assistance with how to deal with distraction or the negative belief pattern that they just "can't do" math. Cooperative learning in math classes can help students learn the math from one another, and also learn how to deal with frustration and to problem-solve. An important SEL contribution of the math teacher is to reflect with students on the skills involved in problem-solving and occasionally ask them to consider how those skills can be used in life outside class as well.

Drama.

Perhaps more than any other discipline, drama provides opportunities for students to harness their emotions and channel them toward a positive end. They develop their expressive communication skills while working together to produce dramatic and musical productions. Student involvement in improvisational humor helps them develop the capacity to relax, be spontaneous, and laugh at themselves. The drama teachers and students at two Arlington, Virginia, high schools currently are developing a project in which they will write, direct, and film short vignettes that illustrate SEL principles.

English.

Most teachers of English correctly believe they already promote social and emotional learning while teaching language and literature. Many, however, forget to state explicitly, both before and after a lesson, the social/emotional principle under consideration, thereby risking the possibility that students will miss this aspect of it. This "highlighting" of SEL principles is essential for most students' understanding. Teachers might consider with students how the theme of the literature or film relates to their lives. What are the short- and long-term consequences of the literary character's decisions? Would students have taken the same course of action? Is there one character with whom students particularly related? Why? How do they control their emotions when in a situation similar to that of the character the class is analyzing? What suggestions can they offer to each other?

- Make use of individual and collaborative reading and response journals. Select questions and topics for these journals carefully: In what situations did a character show empathy? Select one lesson you learned from the life of the fictional character and apply it to your own life and relationships.
- Have students write a criticism of their own work, and make use of peer evaluation of writing. How can we learn to accept criticism without getting angry? How do we provide and respond to praise (and criticism)?
- Use literature that addresses cultural, ethnic, gender, and socioeconomic diversity, and activities that recognize learning differences.
- Utilize group discussions to help students learn the skills of listening, patience, and tolerance while listening to others with different perspectives.
- Discuss the importance of self-awareness in responding to media messages: What emotions is a particular ad trying to elicit, and is it successful?

Foreign Language.

No activity lends itself more naturally to an appreciation of different cultures and backgrounds than the study of foreign language. Language teachers often devote attention to different cultures and the cultural differences between languages. Students can consider how the difficulty we have in learning a new language sensitizes us to the challenges faced by individuals from cultures other than our own. Teachers can examine the need for self-discipline, practice, and self-control in dealing with the frustration of learning a new language. Teachers can build self-awareness and self-esteem by pointing out the skills students already possess in speaking their native language. Teachers also can provide structures for skits and stories that reinforce principles related to multicultural sensitivity. They can consider with students the way feelings and emotions are built into the target language, and can analyze cultural stereotypes with students and discuss why stereotypes of groups are popular.

Teachers can set up varied scenarios where students need to practice the language under study, but also must consider the variety of skills needed in different social interactions. The class can observe a role-playing situation in which a student speaks to a friend, then to her boss; another situation has the student helping a person in distress or dealing with a child. What are the different verbal and nonverbal behaviors used by the student? Were they appropriate? Would they be appropriate in a different context, but not in the role-playing situation demonstrated?

Health Science.

In schools where SEL lessons are integrated into all disciplines, there should be a special link with the school health program. In health and health-related classes, students can receive instruction and practice in strategies that will increase the likelihood that they can handle the varied problems they will likely face as they go through childhood and adolescence. Teaching social and emotional skills is just one part of a comprehensive health program designed to give students the information they need to make wise decisions in the face of peer pressure and violence, disease and substance abuse. Through the use of experiential learning (e.g., cooperative learning, role-playing debates, etc.), students have the opportunity to develop self-esteem as they build competence. The stakes are high, and more than ever students need the skills and information that they can learn in a first-rate health education program.

Science.

Science education today tends to be experiential, which lends itself to the incorporation of SEL lessons. Ask students to think about how the "scientific method" can provide helpful guidelines for other kinds of problem-solving outside the science lab. At times, after completing more engaging lab experiments, discuss with students how the skills they brought to scientific discovery also can help them arrive at other thoughtful answers to problems and situations they will confront in their lives.

Emphasize from the first day how students should—and should not— approach their cooperative, investigative work together. Ask students to consider with you what guidelines are essential for groupwork and cooperative projects in the science lab. Consider with them what makes for successful and unsuccessful solutions to lab projects; once again, on occasion try to draw a parallel with their lives outside the lab. When is attempting something worthwhile, even if one ultimately does not succeed at the endeavor? What are the parallels between problem-solving in science and problem-solving in life? What cooperative strategies enhance or impede problem-solving?

When teaching principles of genetics and evolution, part of the lesson can be used as a springboard to consider the biological source of diversity.

Throughout the year, the teacher should emphasize the importance of listening skills in gathering data, making observations, and following directions.

Hands-on experiences such as labs and science fairs provide students with excellent opportunities to learn not only the skills necessary for the design and creation of a project, but also how to accept praise and constructive criticism.

Business Education.

The business community today recognizes the importance of employees who possess social and emotional skills. Students studying business need to know that employers today are more interested in employees with SEL competence than they are in those with solely academic skills (U.S. Department of Health and Human Services, 1996).

Experiential learning in business class can emphasize and focus on the personal and communication skills needed for effective groupwork and the human relations skills needed by effective managers. Students can study examples illustrating the importance of the need for self-control and the ability to deal with frustration in approaching a range of business problems.

Opportunities to consider and practice steps in decision-making present themselves when students are examining issues related to ethical practices in business. What examples and practices of leaders and businesses demonstrate social responsibility and caring for others, even in the face of concern about the bottom line?

The teacher can explore a systematic approach for solving business problems and encourage generalization to other issues related to student lives.

For many young people, the classroom has become the most positive place in which they are involved with their peers. As educators, we have a primary obligation to help them achieve academically. When we incorporate SEL into our class content and pedagogy, however, we also help them deepen their emotional learning and develop social competencies. In this way, we are privileged to make a positive contribution to both the individual young people we serve and our society at large.

7 Conclusion: It Can Be Done

*We are what we do, and may do as we choose. Often we
do not choose, but drift into those modes which eventually define us. Circumstances push and we yield. We did
not choose to be what we have become, but gradually, im-
perceptibly became what we are by drifting into the doing of those things we now characteristically do.*
　　　　　　　　　—Allan Wheelis, *How People Change*

It would be naive today to suggest that it is an easy task to create a caring
and respectful, self-disciplined and self-motivated community of learners in
many of our schools. The challenges educators face in promoting such communities are as varied as the many societal pressures our students contend
with each day.

Promoting a positive, challenging SEL program in a school is neither
a quick fix nor an easy answer to the many issues young people face. It requires ongoing reflection and adjustment, and a long-term commitment to
help students develop all of their potential as individuals.

With social/emotional learning programs, the starting point must be
individuals within the school who are committed to the value of SEL and
are willing to work with the inevitable stumbling blocks that impede the
development of most new programs.

If there seems to be significant resistance to the project, this must be
addressed first. School staff interested in an SEL initiative must possess a
high degree of persistence, commitment, and patience. Following are some
questions worth considering as you start:

- Does the school community appreciate the fundamental goal: to teach
  children to be respectful and caring individuals within a positive and nurturing learning community?
- Is the introduction of an explicit program in social and emotional education seen as a priority?
- Is there adequate support from the major participants—including formal
  and informal leaders—for the initiative?

- Do administrators, faculty and parents understand the purpose and advantages of introducing such a program?
- Have you sought substantial input from those who must adopt the program in the school and/or their classrooms?
- Have you helped people address their personal concerns about program implementation and assured them of ongoing assistance and support once the program has begun?
- Has interest in the program grown or decreased since the initial small-group, faculty discussions?
- Are the administrators involved and visibly committed to the program?

Once you have established a certain amount of support for SEL within the school, the specific tasks involved with program implementation are much more manageable. Whatever educational opportunities are developed, how can repetition and practice be built into students' daily routine? Can students be involved in designing some of these experiences? How can you integrate the SEL curriculum and programs with other services the school already provides?

Administrators ordinarily commit topics and dates for professional development before the school year begins. When will professional development opportunities be scheduled to ensure that all faculty and staff are aware of the goals of the schoolwide SEL program, and that teachers have the knowledge they need to teach social and emotional skills? Schedule a specific time at the end of the first year to review, change, and enhance SEL activities and programs; ensure that someone is responsible for monitoring and evaluating efforts *during* the school year.

In these days of budget constraints, it sometimes seems it is more important for a school to look good because of favorable statistics showing high math scores, high graduation rates, strong median S.A.T. scores, and the like, than it is to consider its less measurable, but no less real, successes in helping individuals become better educated individuals, capable of making healthy and intelligent decisions. In school, students need to learn the importance of striving for excellence in *all* important areas of life; surely this includes the social and emotional domains in conjunction with the academic.

In developing a schoolwide program, we must seek to involve from the start all those who will be asked to help implement the plan itself. This inclusion will build the responsibility and commitment to the program required by all involved in it.

As educators, we should not expect our work on the development of social and emotional skills in young people to be easy. Schools that expect overnight and easily achieved results will likely be disappointed.

At the same time, directing our educational efforts toward encouraging our young people to develop SEL *and* cognitive skills throughout life seems the wisest thing we can do, for the many reasons that have been discussed earlier. The messages our school environment sends to young people, and the behaviors it encourages and discourages, can be enhanced by our collective efforts in schoolwide and classroom-infused programs.

I believe developing the social and emotional intelligence of our students is a goal within the reach of every school. This will require each of us, as adults, to pay attention as well to our own growth and development in this area. That's just one other advantage of this important initiative.

In the end, every school community that makes a sustained effort in this area has so much to gain, while providing its students with a solid foundation for respectful, responsible behavior—today and for the rest of their lives. I firmly believe that individuals who commit themselves to establishing SEL programs in their schools are significantly enhancing the education they provide the students in their charge—and potentially enriching their own lives in more ways than they probably realize. If you are one of these people, I wish you every success, and firmly believe that our students, desperately in need of your efforts and initiative in this area, will have more constructive, more balanced, and happier lives as a result.

Appendix:
Selected Resources

CASEL, housed formerly at Yale University and currently at the University of Chicago, serves as a clearinghouse for programs and ideas related to social and emotional education programs. CASEL's specific goals include the promotion of social and emotional development in youth, the dissemination of information on social and emotional learning programs, and the education of public administrators in programs and practices that advance school-based social and emotional learning.

To become part of CASEL's mailing list, and request literature that also might help you in organizing a program and specific activities, write to CASEL at the Department of Psychology, University of Illinois at Chicago, 1107 W. Harrison Street, Chicago, IL 60607–7037, or visit their Listserv at majordomo@cfapres.org.

If you have not already done so, take the time to read Daniel Goleman's *Emotional Intelligence*; the bibliography contains a large selection of additional resources on this topic. *Promoting Social and Emotional Learning* by Maurice J. Elias and others is a comprehensive look at all aspects of developing, implementing, and evaluating SEL programs. Other resources include:

(See References for a more complete listing of relevant books and articles.)

Elias, M. J. (1997). *Promoting social and emotional learning*. Alexandria, VA: Association for Supervision and Curriculum Development.

Elias, M. J., Tobias, S. E., & Friedlander, B. S. (1999). *Emotionally intelligent parenting: How to raise a self-disciplined, responsible, socially skilled child*. New York: Harmony Books.

Goleman, D. (1996). *Emotional literacy: A field report*. Kalamazoo: Fetzer Institute of Kalamazoo, Michigan.

Lantieri, L., & Patti, J. (1996). *Waging peace in our schools*. New York: Beacon.

Lazarus, R. S. (1994). *Passion and reason: Making sense of our emotions*. New York and Oxford: Oxford University Press.

Pasi, R. (1997). Initiating a program in social and emotional education. *NASSP Bulletin, 81*, 100–105.

Research and Guidelines Committee of the Collaborative for the Advancement of Social and Emotional Learning. (1997). *Fostering knowledgeable, responsible, and caring students: Social and emotional education strategies*. Alexandria, VA: Association for Supervision and Curriculum Development.

Salovey, P., & Mayer, J. D. (1990). Emotional intelligence. *Imagination, Cognition and Personality, 3,* 185–211.

Salovey, P., & Sluyter, D. J. (Eds.). (1997). *Emotional development and emotional intelligence: Educational implications.* New York: Basic Books.

Sheldon, C. (1996). *E.Q. in school counseling.* Spring Valley, CA: Innerchoice Publishing.

Weissberg, R. P., Gullotta, T. P., Hampton, R. L., Ryan, B. A., & Adams, G. R. (Eds.). (1997). *Healthy children 2010: Enhancing children's wellness.* Thousand Oaks, CA: Sage.

Weissberg, R. P., Kuster, C. B., & Walberg, H. J. (Eds.). (1998). *Trends in the well-being of children and youth.* Thousand Oaks, CA: Sage.

Zins, J. E., Travis III, L. F., & Freppon, P. A. (1997). Linking research and educational programming to promote social and emotional learning. In P. Salovey & D. J. Sluyter (Eds.), *Emotional development and emotional intelligence: Educational implications* (pp. 257–274). New York: Basic Books.

The May 1997 issue of *Educational Leadership*, (published by the Association for Supervision and Development) is devoted exclusively to social and emotional learning.

Lessons for Life: How Smart Schools Boost Academic, Social and Emotional Intelligence (1999) is a three-part video on creating and maintaining SEL programs within schools. It is available from the National Center for Education and Innovation, Bloomington, Indiana.

The PATHS Curriculum is perhaps the best available elementary classroom-based program designed to promote self-awareness, self-control, and problem-solving skills. For more information about the PATHS Curriculum, contact Developmental Research and Programs, 130 Nickerson Street, Seattle, WA 98109.

A number of organizations maintain web sites devoted to SEL:

Board on Children, Youth, and Families. Listen to workshops and read reports on youth development and early childhood intervention at: http://www.nationalacademics.org/cbsselboycf

Collaborative for the Advancement of SEL: www.CASEL.org

Quality Parenting Project of Psychological Enterprises: www.EQParenting.com

Finally, you might speak with your school's library and media coordinators about the possibility of adding educational materials on social and emotional learning to the school's professional library.

References

Adams, D., & Hamm, M. (1994). *New designs for teaching and learning.* San Francisco: Jossey-Bass.

Association for Supervision and Curriculum Development. (1997, May). Social and emotional learning [Special issue]. *Educational Leadership, 54*(8).

Carnegie Council on Adolescent Development. (1989). *Turning points.* Washington, DC: Carnegie Corporation.

Cohen, J. (Ed.). (1999). *Educating minds and hearts: Social emotional learning and the passage into adolescence.* New York: Teachers College Press.

College Board. (1999). *Reaching the top: A report of the national task force on minority high achievement.* Princeton, NJ: Author.

Committee for Children. (1994). *Second step: A violence prevention curriculum.* Seattle: Developmental Research and Programs.

Elias, M. J., & Clabby, J. F. (1992). *Building social problem-solving skills: Guidelines from a school-based program.* San Francisco: Jossey-Bass.

Elias, M. J., Gara, M., Schuyler, T., Brandon-Muller, L. R., & Sayette, M. A. (1991). The promotion of social competence: Longitudinal study of a preventative school-based program. *American Journal of Orthopsychiatry, 61,* 409–417.

Elias, M. J., Zins, J. E., Weissberg, R. P., Frey, K. S., Greenberg, M. T., Haynes, N. M., Kessler, R., Schwab-Stone, M. E., & Shriver, T. P. (1997). *Promoting social and emotional learning: Guidelines for educators.* Alexandria, VA: Association for Supervision and Curriculum Development.

Goleman, D. (1995). *Emotional intelligence: Why it can matter more than IQ.* New York: Bantam Books.

Green, R. (1997). In search of nurturing schools: Creating effective learning conditions. *NASSP Bulletin, 81,* 17–26.

Hawkins, J. D. (1997). Academic performance and school success: Sources and consequences. In R. P. Weissberg, T. P. Gullotta, R. L. Hampton, B. A. Ryan, & G. R. Adams (Eds.), *Healthy children 2010: Enhancing children's wellness* (pp. 278–305). Newbury Park, CA: Sage.

Hawkins, J. D., Catalano, R. F., & Associates. (1992). W.T. Grant Consortium on the school-based promotion of social competence. In *Communities that care: Action for drug abuse prevention* (pp. 64–105). San Francisco: Jossey-Bass.

Kusché, C. A., & Greenberg, M. T. (1997). *The PATHS Curriculum.* Seattle: Developmental Research and Programs.

Lambert, L. (1998). *Building leadership capacity in schools.* Alexandria, VA: Association for Supervision and Curriculum Development.

Mayer, J. D., & Salovey, P. (1997). What is emotional intelligence? In P. Salovey &

D. J. Sluyter (Eds.), *Emotional development and emotional intelligence: Educational implications* (pp. 3–22). New York: Basic Books.

Pasi, R. (1997). Success in high school—and beyond. *Educational Leadership, 54,* 40–43.

Payton, J. W., Wardlaw, D. M., Graczyk, P. A., Bloodworth, M. R., Tompsett, C. J., & Weissberg, R. P. (2000). Social and emotional learning: A framework for promoting mental health and reducing risky behavior in children and youth. *Journal of School Health, 70*(5), 13–19, 179–185.

Ralston, F. (1995). *Hidden dynamics: How emotions affect business performance.* New York: American Management Association.

Stone, K., & Dillehunt, H. (1978). *Self-science: The subject is me.* Santa Monica, CA: Goodyear Publishing.

Sylwester, R. (1995). *A celebration of neurons: An educator's guide to the human brain.* Alexandria, VA: Association for Supervision and Curriculum Development.

U.S. Bureau of the Census. (1997). *Statistical abstract of the United States.* Washington, DC: Cahners.

U.S. Department of Health and Human Services. (1996). *Trends in the well-being of America's children and youth.* Washington, DC: Author.

Vaillant, G. E. (2000). Social and emotional intelligence and mid-life resilience in school boys with low-tested intelligence. *American Journal of Orthopsychiatry, 70,* 215–223.

West, M. L. (1963). *The shoes of the fisherman.* Boston: G. K. Hall.

Wheelis, A. (1973). *How people change.* New York: Harper & Row.

Zins, J. E., Elias, M. J., Greenberg, M. T., & Weissberg, R. P. (2000). Promoting social and emotional competence in children. In K. M. Minke & C. G. Bear (Eds.), *Preventing school problems—promoting school success: Strategies and programs that work* (pp. 71–100). Bethesda, MD: National Association of School Psychologists.

Index

About the Author

Raymond J. Pasi is principal of Yorktown High School in Arlington, Virginia, and a member of the faculty in the Graduate School of Education and Human Development at George Washington University in Washington, DC. A school psychologist and counselor, he also holds a doctorate in Educational Leadership. He is a member of the Educator Prep group of the Collaborative for the Advancement of Social and Emotional Learning (CASEL), and the Advisory Council for the National Association of Secondary School Principals (NASSP). Dr. Pasi has conducted numerous workshops, in the United States and abroad, on SEL and school climate. He may be contacted at *rpasi@arlington.k12.va.us.*

Parent-Friendly
Early Learning